"...I believe that every woman in America has the opportunity to 'be somebody.'"

Coming from a vibrant career woman, such a statement is not at all surprising. That is, until you discover the circumstances that once hampered her from without—and the feelings of inferiority and failure that once haunted her from within. Originally published under the title THINK MINK!, here are the heartfelt experiences of a woman who has truly overcome—and the overwhelming reasons why YOU CAN TOO.

By Mary C. Crowley

Think Mink!
Women Who Win
You Can Too

MARY C. CROWLEY

YOU CAN TOO

Home Interiors & Gifts, Inc.
Dallas, Texas

This material was previously published under the title Think Mink! *This is an expanded and updated edition of that book.*

Library of Congress Cataloging in Publication Data

Crowley, Mary C
  You can too.

  (Power books)
  Earlier ed. (c1976) published under title: Think mink!
  1. Crowley, Mary C. 2. Christian life—1960–   3. Success. I. Title.
BX6495.C747A36   1980   248'.2   [B]   79–20131
ISBN 0–8007–5028–4

ISBN: 0-8007-5028-4

Thirty-sixth printing, February 1994

Printed in the United States of America

Contents

Foreword by Ruth Graham

Proverbs 31:10–31 could well have been written to describe Mary Crowley.

Women's Lib will have to run to catch up with her. Countries with a production problem would do well to study her methods. Mary is an imaginative, industrious, infectious, and incredibly generous person.

Even so . . .

In his introduction to *George MacDonald Anthology,* C. S. Lewis writes, "He [MacDonald] appears to have been a sunny, playful man, deeply appreciative of all really beautiful and delicious things that money can buy, and no less deeply content to do without them."

Would Mary be? Yes. For although Mary's greatest joy in getting is not to keep, but to share with others, if she could not share financially with others, she would continue to share what Christ means to her and to give of herself.

Since getting to know Mary several years ago, our home has never been without either a potted plant or a lovely bouquet of flowers from her. Some time ago I was in a home and admired the floral arrangement. "Mary Crowley sent it to me," my hostess explained. I wondered how many other homes throughout the nation have received Mary's gracious touch.

Yet if Mary went bankrupt tomorrow she would still be sharing with others, for she draws from that inexhaustible supply of love and joy which comes from God Himself. We may not have Mary's business gift, but we have her same inexhaustible supply to draw from and that—Mary would be the first to say—is what it's all about.

RUTH GRAHAM

Thus saith the Lord, Let not the wise man glory in his wisdom, neither let the mighty man glory in his might, let not the rich man glory in his riches: But let him that glorieth glory in this, that he understandeth and knoweth me, that I am the Lord which exercise lovingkindness, judgment, and righteousness, in the earth: for in these things I delight, saith the Lord.

Jeremiah 9:23,24

Editor's note: The Scripture above is lettered on the front wall of the "Chapel in the Wood" at the author's home.

1
When a House Is Not a Home

As I drove up to the house where the party was to be held, my heart sank. I saw weeds filling the flower beds, shrubs growing up over the windows, a broken step crumbling on the front porch. As I carried my two heavy sample cases up the walk, I could spot fingerprints advertising their message of dirt and neglect around the doorbell.

How could I sell a beautiful porcelain figurine, a scented candle, a gilded mirror, or a whimsical plaque in a house that had dirty fingerprints like that?

And when Betty answered the doorbell, I was even more dismayed. She was wearing the black toreador pants that were so popular back in the late 1950s. Her white shirt had a gravy stain on it. When she reached to open the door, I saw a ripped seam in her sleeve.

"It's good to see you, Betty," I said, patting the head of her five-year-old daughter who was peeking out from behind her back. "Are you girls ready for the Home Interiors and Gifts show?"

"I guess so," she said, "but I'm afraid there won't be very many guests. I just didn't know very many people to call."

"Oh, that's all right," I said. "We're going to have a good time." But as I walked into the living room, I was asking myself, *Mary Crowley, how do you get yourself into messes such as this!*

After all, Betty hadn't really volunteered to be a hostess for me. She had attended the last gift show at which I was the Home Interiors Displayer. As I showed the guests how to use the accessories I sold to create a more beautiful home for themselves, the other women had asked questions about their decorating problems. They'd traded their favorite stories about their children and their husbands. They'd laughed and had a good time.

But Betty sat at the back of the room, her long, brown hair straggly, her eyes blanked over with something that looked like helpless resignation. If I addressed a question to her and called her by name—something I often do to draw out shy people—she would answer, "I don't know," or, "I never thought about that."

At the end of the show, as the guests were placing their orders, I presented the hostess with a beautiful framed picture that would fit perfectly in her home. I explained that I always gave hostesses a lovely gift as their reward for inviting me in to show the decorative accessories I sold to their friends.

As I did at every show, I asked if any of the guests would like to be a hostess and let her own friends see our delightful accessories. I'm pretty persuasive. Almost always at least two guests booked a future date with me.

That night I saw Betty sitting alone, saying nothing, with that faraway look on her face. Almost as a gesture, I asked, "Betty, would you like to be a Home Interiors hostess?" Her eyes dilated and she almost smiled. Her hand flew nervously up to her throat.

"Why, yes," she whispered. "Yes, I think I would."

So here I was in Betty's living room, and it was a mess. I wanted to set out my pictures, plaques, figurines, and candles on top of her TV in an attractive arrangement. But first I had to gather up a collection of unpaid bills and try to keep from sneezing as I removed a dusty doily.

"Kathy, will you please take these to your mother in the kitchen?" I asked, handing the bills and doily to the child, whose big brown eyes were watching my every movement. "And ask her if she has a dust cloth."

In a moment, Betty was back apologizing.

"I'm sorry the house is such a mess," she said. "It's just that I seem so tired all the time, living in this place." I stopped dusting and studied her face.

"Honey, I just knew something was wrong," I said. "What *is* the matter?"

"It's Texas," she said, putting her hands over her eyes. I saw her shoulders beginning to tremble. "I've hated it ever since we moved here."

"Honey, I'm sorry about that," I said. "Don't you have some friends who can help you? Friends help a lot."

"No, I don't know too many people here. Just the neighbors—and they certainly aren't very friendly."

"Well, what about your church? Where do you worship?"

"Oh, we haven't gone to church since we moved here."

"When did you come to Texas?"

"Eleven years ago," she said, and she was really crying now. "Eleven years, three months, and nine days."

"Eleven years?" I said. "Why, honey, do you mean to tell me you haven't found a church in eleven years? Do you mean that this precious little Kathy doesn't get to go to Sunday school and meet friends? Oh, please take her." Kathy twisted her corduroy suspenders and grabbed her mother's hand.

"Can we, Mama?" she begged. But Betty pushed her aside.

"I'm too busy. We can't talk about that now," she said. She snatched the dust cloth from my hand and began rubbing the tables with all her strength.

We plumped up the pillows on the sagging sofa and straightened the magazines on the coffee table. By the time the guests arrived, the living room was clean, if not especially inviting. I've found that when a woman is depressed, when she doesn't feel loved, her home shows it as much as her own personal grooming. And Betty seemed as depressed a person as I've ever seen.

We only had five guests that afternoon. Each one was a carbon copy of Betty—slovenly, tired, uninterested in what I said.

"The home should be a haven . . . a place of refuge, peace, and harmony . . . a place of beauty. No home in America ever need be dull and unattractive," I told them. It was as though I were talking to a convention of robots. They just couldn't seem to believe that they could have a warm, inviting home, a loving husband, happy children.

The commission from that party was slim. But I promised Betty that when her order arrived, I would come back and help her hang the sconces and pictures in an attractive arrangement over the sofa.

As I drove away, I wondered if I had helped Betty and her guests at all. Usually I'm a pretty optimistic person. I've always said that God has blessed me with an extra dose of positive thinking. And I know that when people accept Jesus Christ as their Saviour, there's no limit to the changes He will make in them. But Betty had been in Texas eleven years. She just sat around waiting for things to happen. She hadn't tried to help herself at all. How was God going to turn her around?

I didn't have much time to think about Betty the next few days. I had started the Home Interiors accessories business only a few months before. Sometimes I put in eighty hours a week, holding accessory shows, packing and delivering the orders, recruiting new Displayers and training them, writing our weekly *News From Home,* and working in the office.

In fact, I didn't have a chance to think about Betty until the day I delivered her order. It was a Monday afternoon. As I pulled up to the curb, the front door burst open. Kathy came running out on the porch, a long, red rose in her hand. She shoved it, dripping wet, into my hand.

"Why, what's this, Kathy?"

"It's a present for you!" she said, her brown eyes sparkling. "My Sunday-school teacher gave it to me."

"Your Sunday-school teacher?" I said, reaching out and hugging the laughing child. "What a precious gift!" As I looked over her head into the doorway of the house, I saw Betty standing there. She was smiling, really smiling.

"Yes," she said. "I thought about what you said. We all went to church yesterday." It was then I noticed that the fingerprints around the doorbell were gone. The door simply shone with cleanliness.

And suddenly it occurred to me that God knew just what He was doing when He nudged me to ask Betty to have a Home Interiors show. He was revealing to me that Home Interiors was *more* than a business, more than selling mirrors and porcelain cherubs and children's plaques, more even than making a good living for me and for all the other people in the business.

Home Interiors and Gifts was a way in which God could use me, Mary C. Crowley, to help other women to see themselves as He sees them!

And suddenly I was thinking of a strange sermon I had heard a few years before. My husband, Dave, and I were vacationing in Nassau. Sunday morning dawned bright, sunny, glorious. When we opened the window we could smell the flowers and the sea. As we gazed out over the jumble of colorful houses and shops, we spotted the spire of a church. It looked old and quaint. Yet it simply sparkled in the sun.

"Let's go to that church," I said. "It's close enough to walk."

Dave agreed. No matter where we are on Sunday, we always go to church. Sometimes we go to a Baptist one, which is my denomination, and sometimes we attend a Catholic church, which is Dave's. Sometimes we worship with people we are visiting at their own churches.

When we walked up to the front door of this church we felt we were in for a special treat. A sign in the yard advertised that this very morning was the congregation's one-hundredth anniversary.

Inside the church, we found to our surprise that we were the only white people in the congregation. Now I have had black friends all my life. I think it is a dear experience to worship with other Christians of all races. Once the ushers welcomed us, I felt very comfortable. And I'll never forget the sermon.

An enormous black preacher with grizzled white hair leaned over the pulpit, preaching the anniversary sermon. Over and over, like the waves beating against the nearby beach, I heard him exhort his congregation.

"Be somebody," he said, his booming voice as strong as a rusty tow chain, "God doesn't take time to make a nobody!"

What a challenge! I thought. I wrote it down in my Bible and soon forgot about it.

Now, holding the rose and seeing Betty's smile, I remembered that sermon. Not all of it—just the part about God not taking time to make a nobody. *He really doesn't,* I thought. *It just looks that way sometimes.* And often the people we think are "nobodies" are really "somebodies" who are burying their talents because they have no one to tell them the Good News.

After that day, I often quoted that sermon. "God doesn't take time to make a nobody," I would tell the new Home Interiors Displayers I was training. "Be somebody."

My Displayers were soon quoting my slogan to guests at their own gift-and-accessory shows. Often I could see women changing before our very eyes from disgruntled housewives who felt sorry for themselves to bright, alert women, interested in creating a house that was a home. Many joined our ranks of Displayers and found stimulating careers as independent contractors working part time. Some progressed to full-time management within the Home Interiors family.

As Home Interiors grew, I became more and more interested in helping women find true fulfillment. Once I conducted a poll among our Displayers.

I gave each one a questionnaire that she didn't have to sign. I asked what each thought was her greatest problem concerning her own personality, her home life, and her business.

When the answers came back, I was astonished. From all over the country, the answers returned the same. "I just can't cope . . . I don't feel that I can accomplish anything . . . I don't have self-confidence."

So many of these American women, who had every possible freedom to fulfillment in life, said the same thing. They lacked self-confidence. They felt inferior as *persons,* as wives and mothers, as businesswomen.

I almost couldn't believe it. These well-dressed American women were all "vogue on the outside and vague on the inside." They didn't want to be that way. But they didn't know what to do about it. They certainly were not Thinking Mink—at best they were settling for the "rabbit habit!"

Their low self-esteem was shutting love out of their marriages, creating dissatisfaction in their children, stunting their opportunities for fulfillment in their business.

Since then, we at Home Interiors have made it our goal to build confidence in our women. We have done it by encouraging them to put God *first* in their homes, family life, and careers. I believe it is this goal which has led God to bless us with success. And we have been successful beyond my wildest dreams.

I could not have begun to imagine, the day I heard that wonderful black minister's sermon, that someday I would head a company which sold $300 million at *retail* in a single year—which enabled twenty-five thousand women to find fulfillment and make an excellent living.

I could not have begun to imagine that one day our company would give away $97,000 worth of groceries as an extra Christmas present for the home office's 310 employees . . . that we could donate the use of a ranch to loving people who minister to problem boys . . . or underwrite $50,000 in scholarships to the Fellowship of Christian Athletes.

I would not have believed that one day I would be invited to the White House itself to help advise the President of the United States.

But I believe it now. And I believe that every woman in America has the opportunity to "be somebody."

After all, there were plenty of times in my life when it might have seemed, to an outsider, that I was nobody—just nobody at all.

2
In the Beginning

"Mama, Papa, Mama, Papa, Mama, Papa," cried the wheels of the train as I hunched myself against the window and stared at the mountains appearing on the horizon. When the whistle moaned into the wind, a lump pressed against my throat. I felt so weak I could hardly swallow it back.

I was no longer hungry, as I had been the first day on the train. Now I just felt tired. My legs, too short to reach the floor, dangled as helplessly as the cloth legs sewn to my rag doll's body.

"Now, Mary, the porter's coming with a sandwich and a soft drink. You know you like that," said the Woman. I would never call her "grandmother." She was not my real grandmother.

I turned my face to the window and pressed my forehead against the coolness. "Mama, Papa," wailed the wheels.

"Well, little lady, looky here at this sandwich," came the porter's booming voice. "It's chicken. Um, um, don't that smell good?"

I thought of the chicken and dumplings my real grandmother had taught me to fix—the dumplings fluffy as clouds floating in the golden goodness of the broth. My mouth watered. I turned and looked at the sandwich resting in the porter's big hands. In his gold-buttoned uniform he looked like a soldier to me, his dark face gleaming the way my mama's polished parlor furniture did. He was smiling, but his brown eyes were crinkled up with concern.

The Woman was looking at me, too. She seemed to be trying to smile. Her lips made an eggshell crack in the powdery whiteness of her face.

"I don't want it," I said. "I'm not going to eat it!"

"But child," said the porter, "it's been three days. You haven't eaten anything!" The Woman pushed the sandwich away.

"She's just being stubborn, porter. Go on, now. She won't starve," the Woman snarled. She glared at me, popped open a magazine, and began to read.

"Mama, Papa, Mama, Papa," sobbed the train's wheels. But the Woman had said I could not call Mama and Papa that. She said they were my grandparents, not my mother and father. She said she was taking me to my real father's house in Washington State. She said that my brother and sister were already there, that my father had a new wife, who was the Woman's very own daughter. I would have to call her Mama.

But I didn't remember my father. I had not seen my brother and sister since I was eighteen months old. I didn't want a stepmother, either. To me, my "real" mother and father were my dead mother's parents.

There was Papa, smelling of tractor oil and wheat fields and pipe tobacco, his strong hands closing around mine on the steering wheel of the chugging tractor. There was Mama, her long, white apron falling to the floor as she lifted me up onto a stool to help knead the spongy bread dough.

It did not seem strange to me that my papa had white hair which he kept snowy by rinsing it in bluing. Age meant nothing to me. I really knew that they were my grandparents. Still, they were to me the only mama and papa I'd ever known. I was their adored child.

I had come to them at the age of eighteen months, after my mother died of pneumonia. My brother, only three months old, was taken by a half-sister of my father. My older sister was taken by another relative. I could not remember them. I, Mary Weaver, was the granddaughter of W. D. and Laura Crain, living as their daughter in a comfortable home on a wheat farm at Sweetsprings near Kansas City, Missouri.

My grandparents had already raised five children on that farm, asking God's blessing before each hearty meal, gathering for prayers in the evening, going to church on Sunday. They depended on the Lord for everything. And He had provided for them well. They had sent each of their five children to college.

"Pawsh" was what I first learned to call my grandfather, because my grandmother called him "Paw." Pawsh was Irish, the only member of the family who had blue eyes. There was always a twinkle in them. I think I gained my self-confidence and belief in my ability to do almost anything from him.

Papa taught me to milk the cows. He was one of the first in our community to buy a car and I was just about the only one who would ride with him. I loved rattling over the rutted roads in that Overland. Sometimes he sneaked me, a small girl with long, flying hair and dark eyes lit with excitement, onto the seat of his tractor. I could see waves of wheat rolling around me like an ocean.

When he did this, Mama would burst out of the farmhouse door, waving her long, white apron and fussing, "Paw, what do you mean by putting that child on a tractor?"

Mama taught me to clean and cook. A little woman, she fairly loved work. When the threshing crews of great, husky farm neighbors and hired hands came, she had me stirring, kneading, and tending great bubbling pots just as a grown-up would. Even though I was only six and a half when I left that farm, I already knew how to cook.

Laziness, my grandmother felt, was a capital sin. Grandmother was English. She had lots of funny little sayings. "The shadow of a dog does not bite," she would say when I was afraid of something. Or, "A closed hand can't receive." Mama was always feeding some poor tramp who was willing to work for his supper or providing a basket for a sick neighbor. From Mama I learned to love both working and giving.

My grandparents believed in discipline, too. From the beginning, I was taught what was right and wrong. But even more important, they showed me that Jesus was my friend. He was always with me, helping me, making good things possible for me.

Psychologists say that a child's first few years are the most important. I was lucky to have had a warm, loving environment with my grandparents. Perhaps, too, God simply blessed me with supreme confidence in myself. I was born April 1, 1915. God must have said,

"This poor child is being born on April Fools' Day. She's going to need an extra dose of confidence." And He was right.

I had always been a smiling, happy child. I can only remember one spanking I ever received. But now, while riding the train to my father's house in faraway Washington, my belief in myself turned into a terrible stubbornness. This Woman had insisted I could not call Mama and Papa by their names. All right, I'd show her. I wouldn't eat a bite until I got to Washington.

But if I had been unhappy on the train, I was miserable in my father's home. There I had to adjust to a brother and sister I didn't know. My stepmother's house was a far contrast to my grandmother's shining and spotless parlor. My stepmother did not seem to know how to clean things. Clothes, books, and magazines were strewn around the living room. Dust monkeys curled around furniture legs.

She couldn't cook, either. My father had given up on trying to persuade her. He was trying to fix the meals himself. When he learned I could cook, I soon was making all the bread and taking care of the kitchen.

My stepmother made all three of us children miserable. I remember my brother and sister and myself all gathering together and praying that she would be taken away. Yes, I am sorry to say we prayed she would die. We didn't really mean any harm to her as a person but we simply needed desperately to have her removed from our lives.

My father was a contrast to my papa, too. A Latin-and-accounting teacher for a consolidated mountain school, he made books seem very important. I did not dislike school. In fact, I was double-promoted twice—a fact that made my life even more difficult, since I was put in classes with children two years older than myself. The academic emphasis in my father's home was different from the happy and warm farm life.

I resented my father, too. I could not believe that he could be so immersed in school activities and test papers that he did not realize how cruel our stepmother was to us.

Often I would have to slip off into the woods by myself, shuffling through the fallen leaves, listening to the birds. There in that outdoor chapel of trees and sky, smelling the green growing things and wild flowers, I would tell Jesus how miserable I was. It was during these years that Jesus really became my friend, a Presence that I could talk with. He was always with me, protecting me.

Because of my early training and my great need, I can truthfully say there was never a time when I did not know the Lord as a real person. Later, as a teenager, I made a formal commitment to the Lord and to my church. But there was no dramatic change in my life. There was never any time I did not know Him.

My stepmother seemed to go out of her way to hurt us children. The year I was twelve, I had been poring over the new styles of coats in the Sears catalog for months. It was the year that bright-colored wool coats, trimmed with beautiful, soft fox furs, were in style. I had never worn anything but my sister's hand-me-downs since I was six. I was determined to have one of these coats—a red one with a fluffy, warm collar.

All summer I picked fruit and vegetables—cherries, spring peas, and apples in the fall—for a few pennies a day. It was hard physical labor, but my heart fairly sang as I did it. *I was going to have my new coat.* I gave the money to my stepmother to order it for me.

Then one day she and my father got in the car and were away all one Saturday afternoon. When they returned, she handed me an ugly brown coat with worn sleeves and out-of-style tassels hanging down the back.

"We found you a coat at the rummage sale, Mary," she said. I stared at the plain, drab collar.

"That's not my coat," I said. "I wanted one with a fox collar from Sears. I gave you the money for it."

"This one will do just as well," my stepmother said. "It's warm and serviceable and won't show dirt easily. It cost five dollars, and we'll use the rest of the money you made for your school expenses."

"I'll never wear that coat!" I screamed. "Never, never, never!" I ran, sobbing, out the door and into the woods. I hated her. What had I done to deserve such treatment?

"Help me, Jesus," I said, surrounded by the falling brown leaves of fall, "never to wear that coat—no matter how cold it gets this winter."

And I didn't. When the temperature got down to forty degrees below zero that winter, the ugly coat hung in the closet. I wore a blazer to school. Amazingly, I never got sick.

But I count as my greatest victory the fact that many years later Jesus enabled me to care for my elderly stepmother and father with forgiveness and love. Both lived into their eighties. It was up to me to provide for them financially, to take time out of my busy life to provide them with the attention they required. I did not gain this victory without a struggle.

"Look what they did to me," I told the Lord. "Where were they when I needed them all those years? You can't ask me to sacrifice my life for theirs."

But it seemed He answered me, "I didn't ask where you were, Mary, when I needed you." People need loving the most when they deserve it the least. Christ gave me the victory over my painful memories—and even gave me joy in caring for them.

I also learned from that winter how badly a person who is hurting can want something beautiful. "Hope deferred makes the heart sick, but a desire fulfilled is a tree of life," says Proverbs 13:12 (RSV). It is easy for me to understand how a longed-for home accessory can build new hope and life in a home with problems.

When I was thirteen, our neighbors realized that my stepmother was not treating us children properly. The juvenile court declared her an unfit mother and ordered that we be removed from her care.

My sister and I were sent to live with my grandparents once more. I was delighted to return. But Mama and Papa no longer lived on the wheat farm. They had moved near Fayetteville, Arkansas, to help my uncle manage one of the first scientifically planned chicken ranches in the nation.

I was enrolled in high school. Though I was two years younger than my classmates, I was taking some college courses on the University of Arkansas campus by the time I was a senior. But I was not happy; I wanted a home I could really call my own.

When I worried about being the youngest in my class, my grandmother would say, "All right, Mary, if you are determined to worry, then set aside Thursday afternoon. Pick a worry room and go sit there and worry. But don't ruin a whole week with it. Worry is a misuse of the imagination."

When I resented what my stepmother had done to me, my grandmother would say, "Every tub must sit on its own bottom. Don't live in 'if only' land." She helped me see that when things happen to you, you can lose only if you react to them rather than using the experience to progress.

But I never felt quite at home at the new school, possibly because I was younger than the others. Soon I met another student with whom I fell desperately in love. I was sure that together the two of us could establish something I had never really had since my first six years— a home of my own. We were married immediately after high-school graduation in 1932.

I was confident. But what I hadn't figured on was the effect of the Great Depression of the 1930s. Couples who married during those dismal times needed an extra dose of responsibility and courage.

The young man I married was a good person but he was immature. He, too, had been reared by grandparents after his mother died, but unlike mine who taught me responsibility, his had been permissive. He was not prepared for the grim reality of supporting a family during the depression—or for the discipline of marriage.

Donnie Joe was born July 5, 1933, and two years later, Ruthie arrived. I loved my children. More than anything in the world, I wanted them to have a happy home, the family life I had not had. But by this time I realized that if Don and Ruthie were to have the bare essentials, it would be up to me to provide them. My husband could not shoulder the responsibility.

Years later, the army and life were to teach him responsibility. Before his death many years afterward, he would come to be what God planned for him in the beginning.

By the time Ruthie was a year old, I knew I would need to find a job outside the home. I had been baking bread and sewing for the neighbors to earn a few cents now and then. I remember making a cotton dress for twenty-five cents—and I was glad to get it to buy food. I needed a job at a time when CPAs, teachers, and bank presidents were all walking the streets looking for jobs—or going on relief. As for myself, I had no marketable skills. Fortunately, I did not know that.

3
Seek and Ye Shall Find

As Donnie and Ruthie toddled in front of me into my neighbor's house, I could smell a scorched ironing board and pinto beans cooking on the stove. This was the smell of the depression. It was the way all our houses smelled. The reason the thirties were called a depression, in my opinion, was that life was depressing.

As for the way things looked, we decorated our homes by choosing between the illustrated calendars given away by the lumberyards and feed stores. Buying a painting that made our hearts sing because it meant something to us was out of the question.

"How long will you be gone?" asked my neighbor. Older than I, she wore her graying hair in a bun. Her patched housedress spelled out defeat. Why was she standing there looking at me with pity?

"Until I find a job," I said.

"By suppertime, you mean?" she asked.

"Oh, I'll be back long before that," I said. I hugged and kissed Don and Ruthie good-bye. As I waved to them from the front porch, I knew that my neighbor did not think I could find a job. *But I did.* I was twenty-one. I no longer had to nurse my baby, so I could leave her if necessary. I was strong and healthy. I had made excellent grades in school.

Always careful about my appearance, I knew that I looked just as professional as people who had jobs. That morning I had washed and ironed my best dress, a pink cotton, and polished my white sandals. In the mirror I had seen a young, pretty girl with a sparkle of excitement in her eyes. And my smile was perfect. I'd practiced ten different ways of asking for a job with a smile.

Sherman, Texas, where I lived, was nothing but a county seat in a farming community in those days. It was just as depressed in 1936 as any other small town. As I walked around the dusty square, however, the ladies' specialty shops, the hardware store, and the five-and-dime all beckoned with the glitter and color of new things—feathered hats for church, shining patent-leather shoes, dresses of printed voile, multicolored ribbons, and glittering new dishes on which to eat. It seemed a wonderful place to be.

I picked out the largest store that had the prettiest dresses in the windows. As I walked into the cool darkness, the clerk who came forward to meet me had henna-colored hair and a face that looked as if it had never smiled.

"May I help you?" she asked.

"I want to see the owner," I said. The clerk's eyes roved from my young face to my carefully pressed dress and the stockings with seams precision straight.

"If you're looking for a job," she said, "it won't do you any good. The store isn't selling enough to pay us as it is. Mr. Jalonick had to let some of the younger clerks go."

"But I'd like to see him anyway," I said. She shrugged her shoulders and pointed up the stairs.

"He's on the mezzanine," she said.

As I walked up to the office, I glanced back at the selling floor. I could see the rows of tables, and clerks standing around with nothing to do. The cash conveyors which the salesladies stuffed with money and sent along wires to the mezzanine office were all lined up idle. Not a clerk was writing a ticket, much less putting money in the tubes, jerking the cord, and sending them zinging up the wire.

I knocked on the office door. Mr. Jalonick, an immense older man with a mustache, looked at me and sighed as I came in. I smiled my nicest smile as hard as I could.

"And what can I do for you, young lady?" he asked in accented English. I took a deep breath.

"Mr. Jalonick, I'm Mary Carter. I'm twenty-one, and my baby's old enough to leave with someone while I go to work. I looked around the square and decided that your store was the nicest in town—so that's where I want to go to work."

Mr. Jalonick stared for so long I could hear a cricket singing in the corner. He twisted his mustache, looking amused and sad at the same time.

"So, you've picked out this store to go to work in," he said. He sighed heavily. "Young lady, have you heard there's a depression on?"

I laughed. "Oh, yes, sir, I have," I said, "that's why I want a job."

"But nobody has money to buy anything," he said. He turned and looked out the window to the floor below. "Take a look at that. The only time anyone even comes to town anymore is on Saturday."

"Then let me work on Saturday," I said. He shook his head.

"I like your spirit," he said. "You're attractive. You smile a lot. But I have no jobs."

"Just let me work one Saturday," I said, "and if I don't sell enough to more than pay my salary, you won't have to let me come back." Mr. Jalonick smiled and threw up his hands.

"All right, all right," he said. "But don't count on a permanent job."

"Oh, thank you, Mr. Jalonick," I said. I could have hugged him. Instead I turned and went down the stairs, determined to be the best salesgirl he'd ever had. I didn't yet know how, but I was determined.

When I opened the door to my neighbor's home, I was so busy down on my knees hugging and kissing Don and Ruthie that I didn't have a chance to tell her the good news. I looked up and saw that she was offering me a cold glass of water.

"It's tiring, looking for jobs, isn't it?" she asked.

"Tiring? Oh, no. I feel wonderful!" I said.

"You do? Then why are you back so soon?"

"I've got a job—for Saturday at Mr. Jalonick's store!"

My neighbor drank the glass of water herself. She just couldn't believe I had a job. Of course I didn't tell her right away that unless I made an awful lot of sales, I would only have the job for one day.

All that week I tried to think of how I was going to sell that much. I didn't know the merchandise as the other clerks did. I had never held a job a single day in my life. How was I going to outsell all those clerks who had worked there for years?

I am convinced that God honors preparation. Prayer is answered, but we have to use our brains, too. Over and over I kept visualizing the store and seeing those empty cash conveyors and asking the Lord to help me. Suddenly, I had an idea.

Everything in the store, was priced at three cents off the dollar— $.97 or $1.97 or $2.97. No matter what a customer bought, she had to wait for her three pennies change while the clerk put her dollar bills in the cash conveyor, jerked the cord, and sent it up to the office.

Then the customer had to wait while Mr. Jalonick tediously counted out the change and sent the tube back down. If there were only a way to get customers to spend three cents more, they wouldn't have to wait. I could write a bigger sales ticket and with the time I saved, I could serve another customer. But what could a customer buy for three cents?

When I walked into the store Saturday morning I spotted the answer. There, close to the central counter, was a rack of thread— hundreds of spools in all different colors, including sturdy whites and blacks. All were priced at four cents a spool.

"For only a penny more, you can have your choice of a spool of thread and *you won't have to wait for your change,*" I would tell each customer to whom I made a sale. "I'm sure you need some thread at home."

Nine times out of ten, the customer did. By the end of the day, I had sold more than even the clerk with the henna-colored hair. Some of the spool racks were almost empty.

"Mary Carter, come here," Mr. Jalonick bellowed after the store had closed. I fairly raced up the stairs to his office.

"I thought you told me you had never worked before," he said sternly.

"I haven't," I said.

"Well, you certainly are a hard worker!" he said.

"You call this work?" I laughed, thinking of the pinto beans and scorched ironing board back home. "I call it fun. I've never enjoyed anything so much in my life."

"Is that how you get them to buy so much?"

"But Mr. Jalonick," I said, "aren't they interested in buying when they come into the store?" He chuckled. His shoulders began to shake and suddenly he was laughing so hard his mustache was flopping like a paintbrush.

"We forgot," he said. "Yes, we forgot people who come into the store are interested in buying. My dear young lady, can you come back Monday morning?"

I had a permanent job. And I loved it. All my life I have loved to work, and this job was no exception. I enjoyed helping people find what they wanted. I luxuriated in their pleasure at having new things. I truly expected them to buy.

I found just as much pleasure waiting on the ones who didn't have much money as the ones who did. One day a farmwife came in with a gunnysack filled with pecans. During the depression, farmers sometimes tried to barter products they had grown for clothing. Most of the clerks were not too interested in helping a customer such as that. Each week, the clerk who sold the most got a prize of one dollar. But bartered goods didn't count.

This woman had a nice, open face, wrinkled and sunburned from days spent in the field. She looked as though she needed some help, so I volunteered my services. It turned out she had nine children to outfit for school. She bartered the pecans but she also had enough cash to make her purchase the store's biggest sale of the day.

Pretty soon I was winning the one-dollar high-sales prize every week. The clerk with the henna hair was jealous. I had to bend over backward to keep her from resenting me. Even today, I find that unsuccessful people often react with resentment toward those who excel rather than trying to improve their own performance.

But Mr. Jalonick soon had the whole staff following my methods.

"Expect the customers to buy," he would tell the dejected clerks. "Smile at everybody. Ask if they need some thread."

Soon he was telling friends around town about how I had come to him saying I had chosen his store for my first job.

"What could I do?" he would laugh. "She was just standing there, a pretty little thing, smiling at me and telling me *she had chosen me.* What could I do? Nothing, but give her a job." And he would burst out with a chuckle.

For the first time in my life, I had money of my own to spend. But the seven dollars a week that I earned, even with a one-dollar high-sales bonus thrown in, did not go very far, even when hamburgers sold for a nickel. Don and Ruthie's food, their shoes, everything cost more as they grew. Somewhere down the line I knew I was going to have to buy school supplies. And what about doctor bills?

No, my wages were just not enough. If I were going to earn enough to support my children as I wanted, then I was going to have to get more education so that I would qualify for a better job. I was good at math, as my father was. If I could go to business college, I might someday become a CPA. And I knew CPAs made good money.

But there wasn't any business college in Sherman. Just one hundred miles away in Dallas, I might have my choice of business colleges. But I didn't have the money for tuition, much less traveling to Dallas. What could I do?

Then I heard about the Rotary Club. Each year this group of businessmen gave a one-hundred-dollar scholarship loan to a deserving student. The fund was really meant for new high-school graduates who were going to college. Somehow, I managed to win it anyway.

That one hundred dollars was enough for me to enroll in a Dallas business college. Later, when I found a job with an insurance company there, I attended Southern Methodist University's evening business courses. During the week I would work and go to classes. On weekends, I returned to Sherman to be with Donnie and work at Montgomery Ward on Saturdays. A wonderful couple in Sherman kept Donnie for me, since he had started school. Meanwhile, my dear mother- and father-in-law (who had remarried) took Ruthie home with them for a year. I was very grateful for their kindness.

Commuting this way kept me so busy that I didn't really have time to think about long-range plans. Perhaps I didn't really want to think about the future. I didn't want to divorce my husband. My religious training and all my inclinations told me that it was wrong. But my husband had shown a great lack of responsibility toward the children. Actually, I was their sole support. As it was, I had to live in Dallas, separated from them.

In 1939, I moved the children to Dallas and hired a wonderful black housekeeper, Minerva, to care for them while I worked.

Seven years before, I had been a teenager, too young to graduate from high school or get married, but sure that I could create a wonderful home for myself. Now I was the divorced mother of two youngsters, holding down a full-time job and trying to better my education.

Lots of people would have said I was a nobody. But I was determined to become a CPA and be a somebody. There were other lessons, however, that I needed to learn. One of the most important was that God will mend even a broken heart—if we give Him all the pieces.

4
The Desire of Thine Heart

There was just no way that I could tithe. Sitting at my kitchen table after the children were asleep, I figured up the stack of bills, my budget for groceries, rent and housekeeper expenses, the bus fare for going to work and to church on Sundays and Wednesdays. If I added 10 percent of my salary to the debit side of my budget, there would be nothing at all left in the miscellaneous column—no money for Christmas presents, books for the kids, or the dentist. Oh, why did children have to have cavities?

"Lord, You see how it is," I prayed. "I want to tithe but I don't have enough to take care of the kids as it is."

The answer, as answers to prayer often are, was not what I expected.

"Well, Mary," it seemed God was saying to me, "it looks as though you're not doing such a hot job of providing for the kids by yourself. Why don't you give Me a chance?"

Why not? But I was no dummy in mathematics. I had made good grades in my night accounting class. I knew exactly how much money was in my paycheck from the insurance company where I processed premiums and claims all day. I had memorized fixed expenses. There were always unexpected things such as dentist bills coming along, too.

"Lord, You know I haven't enough," I argued.

"Don't you trust Me, Mary?" God asked.

"Well, yes, but. . . ." I was literally pacing the floor that night wrestling with an angel. By the time I signed my name on the pledge card for exactly 10 percent of my salary, the clock had already struck midnight and I was exhausted.

But somehow it was a great relief. I didn't know how God was going to do more with nine-tenths of my salary than I could with ten-tenths, but somehow I felt He was going to do it.

I had to tell Minerva about it the next morning. I knew that to tithe, I would have to take that 10 percent out of my paycheck each month and put it in the pledge envelopes before I spent another dime, or I'd never pay that tithe. If I did that, we would almost certainly have to cut back on groceries. And that meant her job would be a little more difficult.

Minerva's eyes became enormous. She threw up her hands.

"Lord have mercy, Mrs. Carter," she said. "I'm going to pray for a miracle because you're going to need it."

But tithing wasn't the only area of my life in which I was trying to take a step in faith. As a single parent working to support my two children, I had plenty of other problems which I needed to let the Lord solve—without my interference.

These were the war years, a troublesome time for everyone. Rationing made shopping difficult. Prices were high. A lot of people had taken jobs at the aircraft factories and were making high salaries. But I had decided to hold on to my secure job-with-a-future at the insurance company. What could I do about rising prices and a fixed income?

My children, especially Don, needed a male influence in their lives. I knew I couldn't provide that. I was determined to raise them in the atmosphere of love and discipline I had received from Mama and Papa. But I got so tired of always having to be the one who said no.

I wanted time to be with my children to enjoy them. But if I were to provide for them, there was always work to be done, courses to study. Life seemed so daily. Today was just a repetition of yesterday's worries.

If I hadn't had the church, I would never have made it. I had joined the First Baptist Church as soon as I moved to Dallas. I loved everything about it—from the old red-stone auditorium that had been built in the 1890s to the members, who seemed the most genuine people in Dallas. I loved to praise and worship on Sundays, the inspiration I got for living my daily life. Soon I was singing in the big choir and teaching an intermediate Sunday-school class.

Doctor George W. Truett was the minister of this big church which was located in downtown Dallas. It was uncanny how often his sermons would hit dead center on the very problems in my life. From my grandmother I had heard many times that the will of God was always right. But somehow that didn't help me. Even if His will never fails, I reasoned, sometimes my will does.

But Dr. Truett helped me see that the will of God is always right and *safe.* That changed the whole picture for me. Any experience we go through, from a broken heart to a mistake in handling our children, can be used by God to help us realize His love. The will of God is *safe.* We can rest in it and not worry. To help me remember that, I put a sign over my mirror that read not only JESUS NEVER FAILS but also JESUS NEVER FAILS ME.

I soon saw, too, that there were promises in the Bible to help mend a broken heart. One that helped me a lot was John 16:33 ". . . In the world you have tribulation; but be of good cheer, I have overcome the world" (RSV). John 14:14 was another: "If you ask anything in my name, I will do it" (RSV).

Couldn't I pray to have any trace of bitterness removed from my heart? I could and I did. When I had a sleepless night, I learned to turn my insomnia over to God. I'd just say, "Lord, You know I've got to get my rest. You worry about these problems. You're going to be up all night anyway." Soon I would be asleep. The next morning problems would have solutions and my hurts would be healed.

In those days I also memorized Psalm 37, verses 1 through 5, and tried to make it the pattern for my life (italics are mine):

> *Fret not* thyself because of evildoers, neither be thou envious against the workers of iniquity. For they shall soon be cut down like the grass, and wither as the green herb. *Trust in the Lord, and do good;* so shalt thou dwell in the land, and verily thou shalt be fed. *Delight thyself also in the Lord;* and he shall give thee the desires of thine heart. *Commit thy way* unto the Lord; trust also in him; and he shall bring it to pass.

I especially liked the words "Fret not. . . . Delight in the Lord. . . . Commit thy way . . . trust . . . and he shall bring it to pass." The longer I live the more I learn that people want help for daily living. What a wonderful pattern for living! It has helped me through "thick and thin" and I have had about forty years of "thin" to fifteen years of "thick." It works—it worked as I was struggling to raise a couple of kids, worrying about money, feeling lonely. This wonderful blueprint for living worked also when I was building a business and needed God's help daily. It works when you are successful in business and you need God's wisdom daily.

Psalm 37 never says that you can escape responsibilities. Victory does not come from escape but from managing life and facing it head-on.

Sometimes it seems terribly "daily" to be facing a hundred little picky, exhausting problems, however. And I learned to make some basic decisions to avoid being overcome.

1. Choose to do the essentials from among the things you want and must do. The essentials, as I see them, are (a) *learning to develop your character in God's image;* (b) *faithfulness in your family life;* (c) *absolute honesty on the job;* and (d) *helping those who need you.*

2. Rid your life of anxiety. Remember, worry never robs tomorrow of its sorrow; it only saps today of its strength. If I felt myself falling into the trap of self-pity, I learned to get up and do something constructive immediately. If I felt tired, I gained energy by telling myself when I got up in the morning that I felt great. If I dreaded an especially worrisome task, I chose to do it first and get it out of the way.

Getting rid of anxiety also means not harboring ill will against anyone. We must forgive seventy times seven as Jesus taught us (*see* Matthew 18:21, 22). And we must learn to let God forgive us, too. Once we know we are forgiven, we are *free to become somebody.*

3. Delight in the Lord. Learn to praise Him at church and in your work every day. Take time to delight in singing, worshiping, and serving others.

I came to learn during those years that once you learn how much you matter to God, you don't have to go out and show the world how much you matter. We can all be forgiven for our mistakes and become free to walk in the truth and light.

After I learned to delight myself in the Lord, to trust Him to solve my problems, I could simply say, "Okay, Lord, it's Your show. This is up to You." Tithing took the worry out of living—the obedience is mine; the miracle is His.

Minerva always said that God proved that for me with a cyclone. We had been eating nothing but cereal and milk for the last week before my paycheck came in every month, because that was all we could afford. We weren't really hungry, and the cereal was nutritious. But Don and Ruthie would sit with me at the table as we filled the pledge envelopes with tithe money before paying our other bills, and Don would grumble, "We sure could use that money for a good steak, or a bicycle, or a movie." I would go on stuffing the money in the envelope, but it took a lot of praying to do it.

And then a cyclone hit the small town of Goose Creek, Texas, practically erasing it from the map. So many claims came into the insurance company where I was employed that I had to work nights and weekends. I was paid time and a half for the extra hours. These extra-fat paychecks enabled us to buy a steak and save for emergencies.

Minerva always told the children, "The Lord saw Mrs. Carter needed more money because she was tithing. So He sent the cyclone." I could never convince her that God would not destroy a whole town just to help me tithe.

But my tithing did cause my children to learn of the importance of the church in my life in a way that was stronger than any words I could have used. While they didn't understand it clearly at the time, the example had its effect. Many years later they were to witness to that effect.

Tithing and economic reality also caused my children to learn to be workers at a very young age. Don got his Social Security card at the age of ten to deliver orders on his bicycle for a local drugstore and to sell peanuts at ball games held at Fair Park. Ruthie helped around the house. Both had real responsibilities in our household because I had to work.

Some of my neighbors told me I made my children work too hard. But I don't regret having done it. We also had good times together, swimming in city pools and participating in the activities at First Baptist Church. As for hard work, I believe that children learn their values in this way.

Today, I believe many overprotective parents have tried to keep their children from undergoing any kind of struggle or hard work. The result has been that they have sought drugs and protest movements as struggles of their own. By teaching children to work hard, you provide them with the tools they need for living.

Truly the Lord did give me the desires of my heart. We had plenty to eat, a home of love and mutual respect. Eventually, I was to have a fine, loving husband and an exciting career in business.

In my lifetime, God has given me the desires of my heart and more. But these desires were not given instantaneously.

I did not at that time clearly see that God was going to give me more than I believed was possible. More often in those days, I was praying, "Lord, I know Don is going to do something great—please make it legal."

5
A True Dwelling Place

"Mrs. Carter, Don's been out during the sermon riding with the street sweepers again!"

The boy shouted out the news and ran before I had a chance to react. But I couldn't be angry with the little tattletale. I had to think of Don, my teenage son, who was supposed to be sitting in church for the Sunday-night sermon.

He had entered the auditorium, all right. I had seen to that. But as usual he had sat at the back, under the overhanging balcony. And since I was singing in the choir, it was a simple matter for him to slip out the back door of that big church without my seeing him.

I'd heard he sometimes hitched a ride with the friendly street sweepers who cleaned up the almost-empty Dallas streets on Sunday evenings. Other times he made play tunnels out of the huge ducts which had been built into our church's floors and walls in pre-air-conditioned days.

First Baptist used to have enormous fans that would blow over huge chunks of ice and send the cooled air up the ducts in a kind of primitive cooling system. Don thought it great sport to climb through these ducts. He had explored the very tip of the steeple, too. And that was supposed to be off limits.

What was I going to do with that child? Without God on my side, I would really have been worried. Now, I believe in discipline for children. Many is the time that I refused to spare the rod. Once, in fact, Don had even run out into the street in front of our house, screaming to the neighbors, "Help! Murder! Police! My mother's trying to kill me!" I really wasn't. I was just trying to catch him and spank him.

39

But I also believe that you have to expect and hope your children will do great things if they are to come through childhood and adolescence into a meaningful adult life. We just have to remember that sometimes kids have to "climb fool's mountain" before that happens.

I hear a lot of parents these days tearing their kids down, telling them how bad, stupid, and dumb they are. It makes me really sad. I think that even when they do something that hurts you, you can still forgive them and believe in them if you let God take away your own anger and frustration. You can discipline and still have expectations, too.

Kids take in unconsciously what you expect of them. I saw this proven when Don was in his twenties. He had been working for IBM as one of the youngest customer-service engineers they ever had. Then he took a leave of absence to work with me in Home Interiors in the early days. He wasn't sure which career he would ultimately follow.

Don was talking seriously about his future. He said, "Well, whatever I do, I know I'll be a success at it. You always told me that when I was a little boy."

How grateful I was that I had automatically told him that! And of course, his work at Home Interiors has been essential to the success of the company. Without a doubt, he is a success.

Back when he was riding the street-sweeping machines, however, that future was completely unknown. I don't claim to have raised my children without making any mistakes. I made lots of them,—but praise the Lord—He overruled them and really turned the kids out great! God has truly been the loving, forgiving, disciplining Father in our home—daily—not just on Sunday.

I'm grateful that the children and I spent many wonderful hours worshiping and serving at our church. At First Baptist my children and I found wonderful Christian models to follow.

I will never forget the influence of Ralph and Marjorie Baker, the finest example of a Christian couple that I could ever have known. I was teaching intermediates when Ralph asked me to teach in the young-marrieds department which he supervised. Ralph was a fun-loving, attractive Christian. I found he just put his arms around the world. He and Marjorie had three children who were about ten years younger than my Ruthie. I loved watching the way they raised their youngsters.

"My kids can do anything they want to do—within this great, big, protective fence we've built around them," Ralph said. He meant the children had freedom to make mistakes if they had to in order to learn to be loving adults. But they were protected from going too far by love.

I was grateful that Don and Ruthie could observe this Christian home. I myself had never had a Christian home life, except for the very early years with my grandparents. I felt my own children had not had a normal, two-parent Christian family experience, either.

An attorney, Ralph was to become a dear friend who helped me immensely in my future business. He was also a dedicated Christian who taught me a lot about how to make the church an important part of my life. Once Ralph had filled in as temporary choir director while we waited for a professional to fill the spot.

When the new choir director arrived, I said, "Well, Ralph, I guess you're going to take a well-earned rest for a while." He just looked up at me with that smile he wore so often.

"No, Mary," he said, "I've already accepted the superintendency of the young-marrieds department. You see, I found a long time ago that if you're not obligated in God's business, the world will take all your time."

His example has been the inspiration for me to continue as a Sunday-school teacher to this day, and to become involved in many other church activities. How easy it would be to let the world of business, civic duty, and home life take all my time! It takes a conscious effort on anyone's part to put God's business first.

In 1948, I was married to David M. Crowley, Jr., a civilian employee of the National Guard. Dave and I had been in love a long time. I had first met him when I worked for the insurance company seven years before. Dave served in World War II overseas for four years—but wrote faithfully daily.

My children knew Dave well. He had eaten many suppers with us, helped them with their homework, gone with us on outings. They seemed to get along very well. I didn't foresee the strain that this new relationship would create.

But once Dave and I were married, Dave and Don began to butt heads. Don had been "the man of the house," for a long time. He wasn't about to give up his responsibility without a struggle. This friction meant I had to be even more sensitive to everyone's feelings. It was up to me to set the atmosphere of love and mutual concern that I wanted to establish.

I think women can express love by making their homes their true dwelling place. Entering in are good, nutritious meals, clean clothes for everyone, and good decoration. Yes, I believe that decor makes a difference because it shows a woman's love for her family.

In addition to all that, the wife has to make the home a place where husband and children are drawn. She is the magnet.

I had always kept a little book titled *What I Learned About People Today.* Each night I would write down incidents that would be helpful for the future. Now I amended the title to read *What I Learned About My Husband Today.* I wrote down the things he liked and didn't like. I tried very hard to please him.

A lot of little things can cause friction in a marriage. I quickly found myself writing in my little book that Dave likes to arrive early for an appointment or a party. I'm more likely to arrive exactly on time— or even a little late. But if Dave and I are catching a plane together, I get myself dressed and to the airport an hour ahead of departure time if that is when he wants to arrive.

I also believe that wives must make their husbands see themselves as someone special—and working wives must make a special effort. Since our Displayers and managers work out of their homes, it can be a temptation for them to see their husbands as an interruption of their work if they happen to arrive home unexpectedly. I myself have had to remind myself that my husband is the king of his house.

Once when Dave came home from the office unexpectedly, I looked up from a deskful of papers and a list of phone calls to be made and asked, "What are you doing here?"

"I live here," he said, with a wry kind of smile.

Since that day, I've made it a point to lay aside my work when my husband comes home. I give him a loving welcome and let him know he's really tops.

After all, the husband must be the head of the house, while the wife can be the neck. You never saw a head turn without a neck. Also, I think you have to lean on your husband on one side—and prop him up on the other.

Women need a lot of reassurance, too. My husband has a lot of wonderful qualities, but the dearest thing to me is that every morning as he goes to work, he tells me he loves me. If I'm not awake, he makes coffee for me and leaves me a note on one of the IBM cards that he now uses in his work as a computer programmer. The note always says, "I love you."

He doesn't carry out the garbage or mow the lawn, *but he tells me he loves me!* That's really what it's all about.

Working as closely as I have with women, I've learned that many wives don't know how to give their husbands happiness. Wives get bored from staying at home with the terrible "three Ds"—diapers, dishes, and debts. They start watching soap operas and let their homes go.

Pretty soon the house is dirty, the clothes are a mess, and dinner is uninspired. Their husbands can't help but become unhappy and do poorly at work. Soon these women start tearing down their men.

One woman came to me once who was really tearing her husband apart. Finally, I said to her, "Honey, if he is the best you can do, don't knock him!"

But seriously, it is up to the wife to take the leadership role in making the home a special dwelling place. Next to her relationship to God, the most wonderful relationship is the one in the home.

I think women need to dress and look feminine, too. We have dress codes in Home Interiors that inspire women to wear dresses, because we are in a feminine business. Actually, many Home Interiors women like to wear long dresses. They are comfortable to wear, look feminine, and provide a lot of freedom in bending over and stooping down.

Displayers do a lot of that, I can assure you.

I'm not saying you have to wear a long dress to look feminine. But it does take effort for you to look your womanly best. A conscious effort is required. Make your husband feel like a king, and you will automatically feel like a queen, as the saying goes.

Our Home Interiors standard for women is:

> Be physically attractive;
> Be emotionally stable;
> Be financially intelligent;
> Be intellectually awake;
> Be spiritually dynamic.

Back when the children were in high school when Dave and I were first married, I longed for more time away from my work in order to make a more attractive home. And I saw plenty of other women who needed more than just time.

By now I was working as an accountant for a large furniture company. Customers would come in, look through a lot of furniture catalogs, and place their orders.

In the late 1940s, veterans of World War II were returning to get married and set up homes as fast as they could. They would come into the offices of this company with severance pay and sign an order for a whole houseful of furniture and accessories at one time. Often I would try to help these veterans and their wives choose furniture they really liked.

"Do you like Early American styles?" I'd ask. Or if they wanted limed oak, which was popular in those days, I'd ask, "What kind of accessories will you use with it? What colors will you use to coordinate it?"

Often these young couples would just look at each other completely perplexed. They had no conception of decorating, yet they were spending money hand over fist on major purchases which in a few short years could cause real unhappiness.

There should be some way these couples could have a decorator's advice without having to pay a big fee, I thought. I helped them as much as I could and put that wish at the back of my mind. At that time the thought was just that—a wish and nothing more.

I had other problems to think about. Don and Ruthie were now teenagers undergoing all the growing pains normal for their age. I had to concentrate on creating a loving atmosphere in my home to draw Dave and the children to it.

If only I had more time, I often wished. If only I could be at home when the children arrived from school. But I was working an eight-to-five job. It was a good, secure job, one in which I could help people with their furniture selections, which in turn would help them create a happier home.

I was so grateful for that job that when the answer to my prayers and wishes came, I almost didn't understand it. I didn't yet comprehend how God could grant me the desires of my heart, even when He offered them up to me right before my nose.

6
Falling in Love
With Direct Selling

It was one of those rare winter nights in Dallas when there was snow. The streets were covered with ice. Since the city usually has no need for snowplows and does not own any, I knew the streets would stay as slick as a skating rink until the sun melted the snowy crust the next day.

But this was the night that one of my Sunday-school young-marrieds had invited me to attend a Stanley party. I looked at the icy streets and almost backed out. But I knew Lea was really struggling on a limited budget. At the Stanley party she would receive a gift, with the value of the prize dependent on the amount of sales made at the party. I could always use waxes and polishes, and my purchases would help her out.

Since Dave was out of town on a training stint for the National Guard, I decided to go. I slid and slithered down the driveway to her walk-up garage apartment. As I struggled up the icy steps on which Lea had sprinkled sand, she opened the door and welcomed me.

"I didn't think anyone would come at all," she laughed.

When I walked into the tiny apartment, I realized just how much a Stanley prize would mean to Lea. The "living room" was also the kitchen and the dining room. An apartment-sized stove, a miniature refrigerator, a table for two, some borrowed folding chairs, and a sofa filled every inch of the room.

Only three people made it to the party besides Mary Kay Eckman, the Stanley demonstrator. She was an attractive blonde woman with a cheerful, positive manner that I instantly liked.

Mary Kay showed us her waxes and polishes and talked about how important it was to keep a clean, shining home for your family.

"A house is not a home unless you make it that way," she said. She seemed to be echoing my sentiments exactly. Soon the six of us were enjoying Lea's cake and coffee and chatting away as old friends would do.

"What kind of work do you do, Mary?" Mary Kay asked me. I told her I was an accountant at Purse and Company but that I also spent time trying to help customers with their furniture selections.

"I really enjoy sales," I said.

"Then why don't you join the Stanley family and be a demonstrator?" Mary Kay asked. "You could have lots of time to be with your children when they come home from school."

"Oh, but I make one hundred dollars a week as an accountant," I said. I was proud of that. In 1949 that was an impressive salary for an accountant. But Mary Kay only smiled.

"So do I—on a bad week," she said. I stared at her. Could she really make as much money selling waxes and polishes at parties as I did working eight to five every day? And even if she did, how long would that kind of career last? If hard times came, people probably wouldn't buy as many waxes. And then where would I be?

"But I need the security of a permanent job," I said.

"You ought to try it," Mary Kay said. "I think you'd be good at it."

I went home from the party with a vague sense of unrest. The idea of selling to other women in their homes really appealed to me. As for sharing God's love, what better way than to be invited into homes where people don't know Him? Why, I could even help women with their home-decorating, too.

But if it didn't work out, where would I ever find another accountant's job that paid one hundred dollars a week?

"You could try it part time," Mary Kay said when she delivered my order. One night after work, I held my first Stanley party at a friend's house. It was every bit as much fun as working at Mr. Jalonick's store! In fact, I liked this kind of selling better because I got to know the customers in a very personal way. Before long I was booking two or three parties a week—and making more than the one hundred dollars I made as an accountant. I quit my secure job-with-a-future and began working full time with Stanley Home Products.

That was the beginning of a lasting friendship with a supersaleswoman, the person who would go on years later to create the Mary Kay Cosmetics Company. The two of us just clicked. We agreed about God's being a God of abundance who wanted us to have lots of good things, both material and spiritual.

"God never made a stingy sunset," I'd point out. "Look what beautiful colors He put into them."

"And the flowers," Mary Kay would add. "He certainly used a lavish hand on them."

"I think God gave us an aesthetic nature just so that we could enjoy beautiful things. And He provides a way for us to have them if we just let Him," I said. "If only everyone could really believe it!"

We could go on for hours that way. I became a top salesperson, and before long Mary Kay's unit made the third-highest sales in the nation. I was making more money than I'd ever made before.

I found out, however, that I really wasn't always at home when the kids arrived from school. Being a full-time salesperson means putting in a full-time workweek. But the hours were flexible. I could reserve important dates if Don or Ruthie had an activity I wanted to attend, then make up the time on weekends.

With my new job, the children had additional responsibilities, too. When I sent in an order for the week's sales, the delivery would be made in bulk—twelve bottles of furniture polish, ten cans of wax, five quarts of wax "Easy Cleaner." Don and Ruthie would separate the bottles and cans into each customer's individual order and deliver it. They had a regular little "warehouse" on my screened porch.

One of my neighbors used to stand at her kitchen window and watch the kids filling sacks. She kept seeing me bustle out dressed in my business clothes with a case of samples under each arm and a smile on my face. One afternoon she stopped me in the yard to talk.

"My husband thinks a woman's place is in the home," she said, patting the curlers in her hair. She was wearing an old shirt that belonged to her husband and wrinkled pants.

"He does?" I said. I was wearing a new dress with a polka-dot scarf and shiny patent-leather shoes with heels several inches high. "I guess I am just lucky. My husband is proud to have a wife with talent and ability that she can share with others." (It's really true. I'm a liberated woman because I have a liberated husband who appreciates me.) But this answer did not satisfy her.

"Well, you wouldn't be half so successful if you didn't use your kids to do your work," she sniffed.

"Oh, but I think it's good for kids to work," I said. "They like it, too, because it gives them a chance to earn some money. And they're really learning how free enterprise works, too."

This woman's attitude did not bother me at all. I was already in love with direct selling.

I thank God that my children did learn to work hard. They have always been workers in everything they do. And they have been givers, too. I don't know whether they learned this or whether God just gave them generous hearts.

I do know that direct selling encourages giving. It just seems that the more you give of yourself, your time, and your talents, the more you are blessed in return.

Now I was an independent contractor, an entrepreneur just as much as a store owner or corporation executive is. I really began to study my Bible, seeking help in how to run that business. The Book of Proverbs especially became my "B.S." in Business Administration. Proverbs is part of the wisdom literature of the Old Testament. And true wisdom is looking at life from God's point of view and seeing ourselves and others as Jesus Christ sees us. This was just what I needed.

Proverbs 3 especially is a wonderful guide for business leadership: "Trust in the Lord with all thine heart; and lean not unto thine own understanding. In all thy ways acknowledge him, and he shall direct thy paths" (verses 5, 6).

I think trust is the important thing—I had to learn this. A lot of times we don't completely trust the Lord. We want to hold back a little piece of ourselves—our anxiety, our selfishness—for our own will. But the Bible says, "Trust in the Lord with *all thine heart*" (author's italics).

That means trusting Him even when we don't understand. How many people miss out on the joy of loving and trusting God because they're trying to figure out how to succeed, how to direct their lives on their own? They just can't let go and let God. It has taken me a lifetime to understand that I didn't have to "understand."

After just a few months, I became manager of my own Stanley unit. Later, Mary Kay married my brother and moved away from Dallas, and I had some of her people in my unit, too. (This marriage was dissolved nine years later, but Mary Kay and I have continued to be good friends.) Then it was up to me to inspire, to settle differences, to encourage, to sympathize in times of trouble. I found a great joy in working with women this way, especially because it meant giving of myself.

In 1954 I got the chance to reach even more women. A new direct-sales company was being formed by an importer who wanted to sell gifts and decorative accessories from many countries. He knew how to import the merchandise but he didn't know anything about training women to sell on the party plan. He came to see me and asked me to become his sales manager.

Even though I was doing well with Stanley, I was challenged by the idea. Those products brought me closer to the desire I'd had all along of helping give decorator advice. But it really meant starting from scratch. I not only had to recruit salespeople and set up his organization but I also had to use my own back porch as an office for three months. Then, when he furnished an office, I had to supply my own desk, chair, and filing cabinet.

Within three years, I had built up a staff of five hundred women selling on the party plan. Mary Kay moved back to Texas and I recruited her into the organization.

At first I was allowed to run the sales organization exactly as I wanted. We gave good commissions to our salespeople. I taught the staff to think of customers and hostesses as people with needs first, and customers second. We had rallies, seminars, and a lot of good fellow-ship. We gave away trips to Mexico as sales prizes for top producers.

One year when I took a group of winners to Mexico City, I discov-ered that the owner had scheduled a cocktail party as one of the activities. I didn't like that one bit and I told him so.

"You can't run the sales department as though it's a Baptist Sunday school, Mary," he said. He let me know he wasn't going along with my wishes anymore—for I was very firm in my belief that alcoholic beverages did not fit in with my purpose in building people.

I tried to continue to work for him. I had had a lot of respect for him in the beginning. But now that our salespeople were just begin-ning to make good incomes, he put limits on how much commission they could make. I felt he was really working contrary to the basic law of abundance that is God's. I wrote a letter outlining my differ-ences with him and saying I would have to resign if changes were not made.

I really felt badly about these differences and hoped he would see things my way. But the following Monday at 7:00 A.M., I heard the sound of a truck in my driveway, and then the ringing of my doorbell. Dave and I arrived at the door at about the same time. It was the man from the company warehouse. "Here's your furniture," he said.

"What do you mean?" I asked. After a fitful night I could scarcely open my eyes, much less understand.

"Your furniture, Mrs. Crowley, from the office. It's yours, isn't it?"

"Why, yes."

"Well, the boss told me you wouldn't be using it anymore," he said apologetically. "He told me to bring it to you."

We told him to put the desk, the chair, and the filing cabinet in the middle of the living room. We couldn't think where else to put them just then. They stood there, empty and meaningless as an abandoned house, a reminder of the beginning four and a half years ago—when both my furniture and my philosophies were welcome and wanted. Now, neither were wanted anymore. I threw myself down on the sofa and started to cry.

7
Birth of a Company

"He can't do that to you!"

My husband, Dave, was just as angry with my boss as I was. In fact, my big, strong, adorable Dave had just offered to beat up my boss! In between sobs, I assured him that I didn't want him to do it.

"Vengeance is mine, saith the Lord!" I reminded him. It was the only verse I could think of at that moment. Dave fussed and fumed but finally he had to go to work.

"Try not to take it so hard," he said as he kissed me good-bye. But the moment he closed the front door, I cried all the harder. It just wasn't fair, I told myself. I'd worked day and night to build up my boss's business. I had tried to work out our differences with dignity, and his sending my furniture out on the truck was an insult.

Also, I had put countless hours of myself into training his people. Now, what did I have to show for it? I would have to find work with another company about which I knew nothing at all, or look for a different kind of future.

Soon all the wasted years with my stepmother, all the hurtful things people had ever done to me, were churning around in my memory. I was about to work myself into a real case of the self-pities.

Then a vision of my grandmother, standing in her long, white apron, flashed into my mind. "Don't live in 'if only' land, Mary," she said.

I'd always told the women who worked with me, "Instead of being an *if* thinker, become a *how* thinker." Now it seemed God was saying, "Don't just sit there and feel sorry for yourself."

And so I took a step that was as important to my life as Columbus's setting sail was to the discovery of America. I dried my tears, bathed, dressed in my nicest outfit. I went to see my friend Ralph Baker.

Ralph was appalled to learn what had happened. He didn't hesitate a minute. He picked up the phone and called a friend who had the perfect solution for me. Then they took me to lunch.

Ralph and his friend wanted me to head up a new women's division for an insurance company.

"It's a top-notch career, just made for you," said Ralph. "You'd be selling to other women, and you'd have plenty of opportunities to help them, too."

"I'll think about it," I said. I thanked my friends for the lunch and left them. Somehow, selling insurance just didn't have the same appeal that direct sales did. I was grateful to know they thought that highly of me. But hadn't a lot of women with whom I worked often urged me to set up my own direct-sales company?

I knew that was what I really wanted to do. If I had my own company, I could set the standards I wanted upheld. I could be as generous as I wanted with the commissions.

What would happen if I started a business that was really dedicated to helping women create happier homes? Wouldn't it just have to succeed? But how could I create such a company? Nobody knew me and I didn't have the capital or the contacts with suppliers. Or so I thought.

On an impulse, I went to call on H. T. Ardinger and Son, a large importer of decorative accessories from the Orient. My ex-sales staff had sold a lot of Ardinger plaques and figurines. But I felt sure the Ardingers themselves did not know me.

When I entered the office, the dignified wife of the importer himself asked if she could help me.

"I'm Mary Crowley," I said, "and I used to be the sales manager for—"

"Why, yes," she said, before I could finish, "we certainly know who you are."

"You do?" I asked.

"Certainly," she said. "But did you say you're not the vice-president and sales manager anymore?"

"That's right," I said. "I wanted to start my own company. And I want to buy from you." Mrs. Ardinger broke into a big smile.

"Horace, come here," she called to her son, who later was to head the Ardinger Company. "Did you hear the news? Mary Crowley's going to start her own company."

Before I could say another word, all the Ardingers were shaking my hand and congratulating me. As self-confident as I normally am, I almost could not believe their response. I had never realized that when you are in business, many, many other people are watching you closely.

The Ardingers not only knew of the high standards I had tried to set but they also approved of them and wanted to help me. Soon they were referring me to other suppliers who could help. I went to see Ward Adams and Rubye Tedder and Son, some of the large south-western representatives of manufacturers all over the nation. These wonderful people simply picked up the phone and called Mark Ross, a West Coast decorative-accessories wholesaler.

"Whatever this girl wants, let her have it," they said. I had not established any business credit at all. Based on my past reputation, these people were willing to sell to me and to act as references.

By the time Dave came home from the office, I was the buyer, manager, and entire sales staff of a brand-new company. Instead of the red-eyed wife he had left in the morning, he now found me bubbling over with exciting plans.

"There's just one thing," I said.

"What do you mean?" Dave asked.

"I'll have to work pretty hard to set up this business. I'll be away a lot of evenings. I may be tired when I do come home. If you don't want me to do this, just tell me and I won't." I have to admit I held my breath.

"Honey," Dave said, "if you don't go into business, the world of business will be the loser."

I will always adore my husband for that answer. If he had not wanted me to begin Home Interiors, I was really prepared to drop the whole thing. We had to be in it together if it was going to work.

I had my husband's agreement, my suppliers, and the outlines of a brand-new company. The day that had dawned with the funeral for my old career was ending with the birth of my very own company. Out of my disappointment came victory.

This experience reinforced a lesson I had learned as a child while living with my father and stepmother. You never gain by sitting around feeling sorry for yourself. Attitude is the mind's paintbrush. It can color a situation gloomy and gray, or cheerful and gay. In fact, attitudes are more important than facts.

The first thing you should do if you have the slightest twinge of self-pity is to get dressed, leave the house, and do something constructive. Take what action you can—and do it immediately.

Sure, there really are times in everyone's life when things happen that just aren't fair. Life is not always fair, but we don't have to give into self-defeat. I like to say that life by the yard is hard—by the inch it's a cinch. Put another way, God leads, not by miles, but by inches. But it is up to us to take the first step, to move that first inch. For me, God had already opened all the doors to a new business, but I had to get up and go through them!

Only ten days after this important day in my life, Home Interiors and Gifts was official. Ralph Baker had gotten the charter for us in record time by "walking it" through the government maze at Austin rather than relying on letters. We had to work fast if we were to begin. My suppliers wanted to start shipping immediately. There were talented salespeople who wanted to join me—if I could set the company up right away.

But I told Ralph, "I don't want to begin this company at all if it isn't what God wants it to be. It has to be right for people everywhere." Ralph agreed.

"What will you use for your guidelines, Mary?" he asked. I thought a minute.

"I've always admired Rotary International's Four-Way Test plaques," I said. "How about that?" We looked at these famous rules:

Is it the truth?
Is it fair to all concerned?
Will it build good will and better friendships?
Will it be beneficial to all concerned?

We both agreed they were perfect.

On the morning of December 5, 1957, Dave, his mother, my family and I, and five or six friends and businessmen who were willing to invest some of their life savings gathered in Ralph's office. I was pleased to know that each person there was an active Christian.

Then, as my heart did push-ups, Ralph was leading us in prayer. I don't remember the exact words, only that he was asking God to lead us and always be present with each of us. He asked that God lead us to make the company right in purpose.

When we signed the papers, Home Interiors and Gifts became a reality. No bells chimed out, no noisemakers popped. But putting my signature on that charter was every bit as exciting to me as hearing the clock chime at midnight on New Year's Eve. I knew we had the beginnings of something great. I couldn't see clearly how everything was going to develop, but I had plans.

I was going to introduce to home decorating a new idea, which we were to term "room concepts." Our customers would never have to buy accessories from direct-mail catalogs or stores, then take them home and wonder on which wall or table to put them, or whether they would "go" with what they had. Instead, we would come into their homes, give them decorator advice slanted for their very own rooms, and help them express their own unique personalities—all with carefully selected, coordinated accessories.

I was going to write a code of ethics that said:

We believe in the dignity and importance of women.

We believe that everything woman touches should be ennobled by that touch.

We believe that the home is the greatest influence on the character of mankind.

We believe that the home should be a haven—a place of refuge, a place of peace, a place of harmony, a place of beauty.

No home in America ever need be dull and unattractive.

We are dedicated to doing our part to make every home have Attraction Power.

We would call our salespeople Displayers because of their special decorator-accessory knowledge. We would offer them a career with unlimited financial benefits. A Displayer would be able to recruit new Displayers to build a unit and become a manager who would receive commissions from her recruits. The manager would not lose commissions if one of her recruits built her own unit. Instead she would share in more commissions. Managers could actually earn unlimited commissions—and many make as much as seventy thousand dollars a year or more.

We would make it fun to work for Home Interiors. We would give away mink stoles, trips to Hawaii, silver bowls, and fifty-dollar bills as sales prizes. We would hold annual seminars to crown as queens the top Displayers and managers. They would wear ermine robes as they walked down the runway to music and the cheers of the audience. Yet we would encourage the right spirit of competition. For the most part, each woman would compete only with herself. She would look on her prize as a trophy of her own achievement.

Suddenly the slogan "Think Mink" popped into my mind—think the best—not rabbit or squirrel—that was it—it would be a real Think Mink endeavor!

But most important of all, we would so lead our women that they would seek their highest fulfillment in helping others.

Many people have helped through the years to bring this dream into reality. I had a fine co-worker who helped greatly in the early years and then left to build another business. Many hands and hearts helped and *it is true,* we really did set up that kind of company. Today, Andy Horner, one of our vice-presidents, has put up a sign in the home office that says, "In most companies, P&L means 'Profit & Loss.' In Home Interiors, that means 'People & Love.' "

It is the ever-present relationship we have with the Lord that has accomplished all these miracles. Back in 1957 on the December morning when I signed the charter, I did not know exactly how all of this would come about. I only knew that we had the love and backing of friends and that God was on our side—and that He would use me if I stayed available.

It was good that I had such strong faith in Home Interiors' future. Like a farmer planting his seeds, I was going to have to wait a long time for the harvest. Before I could fill up the silos with my good grain, I would experience hailstorms, drought, and flood.

8
"Little Housewives"

Two banks had already said no.

I had not asked for very much of a loan. By banking standards, six thousand dollars is definitely a low-priority transaction. But six thousand dollars was the difference between whether Home Interiors and Gifts would continue as a reality or just a dream.

In the few months since we had subscribed the stock, Home Interiors had done very well. Already I had a number of dedicated Displayers working with me night and day. Supplies were coming in briskly and shuttling right back out the one-door warehouse which Don had fitted out with shelving made from salvage materials.

The only problem was a lack of operating capital. I needed to pay my suppliers if I were to continue to order the merchandise which our Displayers were selling so fast. But we had to order in advance of our need. Furthermore, our customers did not pay until the merchandise was delivered. There was a lag between the time a Displayer held a show, ordered the merchandise, delivered it, collected for it—and then sent in the remittance.

The time lag had caught up with us. We had plenty of accounts receivable—that is, money owed to us that eventually would be paid —but not the cash in hand. Besides, we needed the money for sample cases for new recruits.

Big business constantly faces the same problem. Banks compete with each other to make loans for companies who need "seed money." I thought it would be a simple matter to get a loan after reading the billboard advertising and hearing TV commercials such as "Give us a chance to say yes." One bank claimed to have "Silver Star Service."

I chose the bank offering "Silver Star Service." It was the slogan of the largest bank in Dallas and it was where we all banked. I went to see one of their loan officers. He was an older man dressed in banker's gray, who kept turning his glass paperweight upside down, watching the landscape inside the glass turn snowy. I took out my financial statement and laid it on the table.

"But why didn't your boss come to ask for the loan in person?" the banker inquired.

"I am the boss," I said. "I am president of Home Interiors."

"Oh?" the loan officer replied, turning the paperweight upside down again. He barely glanced at the financial statement. "Now let me get this straight. You say your accounts receivable are in the hands of some little housewives who are selling things for you in their homes?"

"They are independent contractors, trained in the business," I said.

"But they work at home."

"Yes, they sell to other women in their homes, at parties," I said. "You can see from my sales projection that your loan would be well covered."

"I'm sorry, madam," the man said. "We really can't give you a loan on a business such as this."

I was turned down but I was not discouraged. The next biggest bank had the slogan "Give us a chance to say yes." At this bank I went to the head of the loan department. He listened attentively but had to make a lot of investigations and I didn't have a lot of time left, for I had to get back out recruiting and training.

People had tried to tell me that women didn't receive bank loans, especially when they headed a staff that was almost all female and which sold to women. Who could expect those women Displayers to be able to handle money, anyway?

I did, for one. As far back as when I was a Stanley unit manager I had learned that women are fully capable of keeping their checkbooks balanced and their business funds separate from their home accounts. Of course, there were always some who had to learn the hard way that it was dishonest to hold Stanley funds to pay their own bills while they waited for their husband's paycheck to come in. And some who were overloaded with debt just never paid at all.

Usually, all I would have to do to get such women straightened out was to call them and ask firmly but kindly, "What is this mess you've gotten yourself into?" Usually, they would break down and cry while telling me all their problems. Together we would work out how they could pay Stanley what they owed. If they promised never to hold out money again, I gave them a second chance. Many of these women learned integrity and became top salespeople.

As for the "little housewives," as the banker called them, he would be surprised to learn what meticulous accountants most become. I had every faith in my Home Interiors Displayers. I think women are really special.

My version of Genesis is that when the Lord created the world, He looked at it and said, "That's good." Then He created man, looked at him, and said, "That's good, but I believe I can do better." *So . . . He created woman!*

Women do have a special sensitivity that most men don't naturally have. By sensitivity, I don't mean moodiness or getting their feelings hurt at the sound of the first cross word. I mean that women have an ability to see into another person, to know what's bothering her—or him—to empathize and want to help, that most men don't have. This plus quality not only helps women become good wives and mothers but it also is a valuable addition to the business world.

I do not feel complimented when men say I think the way a man would. I don't think as a man does because I think the way Mary Crowley does. One of the best things about being a woman is that I don't have to go out into the world and prove I'm a man. I speak from a full cup. I'm deeply glad I'm a woman.

I know there is discrimination against women. I've been the butt of it in many a situation. But I fully believe that when a man discriminates against a woman, it diminishes him, not her. Any female who feels she is being discriminated against in her work should quit her job and find employment with someone who doesn't practice discrimination.

But what do you do when you're a woman and can't get a bank loan?

I walked down the city street with my briefcase full of facts and figures about Home Interiors in one hand and my purse in the other.

Mary, I told myself, *you know Home Interiors is good for everyone involved. You know you dedicated the business to God. Now go see another bank and get a loan.*

Just at that time I glanced up and saw a billboard advertising yet another bank. The Mercantile Bank, third largest in Dallas, claimed to be "the big friendly bank." *I wonder if they mean it,* I said to myself. *I'm going in and find out.* I decided I would go to the very top officer in that bank—R. L. Thornton, Jr., the son of the founder.

I marched over the thick carpet to the secretary sitting at her desk and said, "I'm Mary Crowley. I want about five minutes of Mr. Thornton's time. I want to discuss a proposition with him that will be beneficial to us both."

The secretary's mouth dropped open. Then she turned on her heel and bustled into Mr. Thornton's office. In a minute she beckoned me in. Mr. Thornton, a tall, friendly man with a keen look in his eye, invited me to sit down.

"What can I do for you?" He had a real Texas accent which made him sound almost folksy. While he was obviously studying my appearance, he seemed to have respect.

I immediately got out my facts and figures and showed him the accounts receivable we had and the future projections.

"We need six thousand dollars to invest in future salespeople who will make profits for our company—and your bank," I said.

"What's your own background?" Mr. Thornton asked. He had not said a word about the fact that I was a woman.

I told him about my experience with Stanley and the other company. I let him know I knew I could make Home Interiors into a profitable business. Mr. Thornton simply reached for a loan form and signed it. I, a woman with a new, unknown company, had the loan.

Looking back, I now remember that first year in business as just a blur of eighty-hour workweeks, of driving my car all over Dallas to hold Home Interiors decorating shows, of following highways all over the big state of Texas to train new people, of consulting with suppliers, accountants, and warehouse workers.

It was and is my theory that if you build the people, the people will build the business. If you help other people get what they want out of life, then you will get what you want out of life. I struggled to build this sense of "otherness" into our sales force, and urged all our employees to apply this nurturing attitude to their families as well.

A lot of women I recruited into Home Interiors had never held a job or gone to college. Most were completely dependent on their husbands for support while they put their energies into raising children. Some had neglected their appearance to the point of dowdiness.

How was I going to turn women such as those into well-groomed, radiant Displayers, knowledgeable about home-decorating, able to relate to other women with poise and confidence?

First I helped them overcome their fear of speaking before an audience. "If you went to town and bought a new dress, would you be able to come home, sit down over a cup of coffee with your neighbor, and tell her what it looked like and why you liked it?" I would ask. Inevitably the answer was yes. "Holding a Home Interiors show is much the same. You just talk to one person at a time within the group, telling her about something you like—the Home Interiors accessories."

I tried to teach each new Displayer to look at everyone, from the hostess on down to the most negative guest, with the *eyes of love.* "See the person as God sees her, a valued child of God, the person she might be able to become, not necessarily the way she acts at the moment."

I tried to show these new recruits that they should be alert to the needs of other women. "Service is our survival kit." We needed to give service in home decorating and we also needed to allow troubled women to air their problems and express their hopes and fears. I encouraged my Displayers to help in whatever way they could.

When I first began Home Interiors I coined the phrase "Think Mink. Think the Best. Don't think rabbit, fox, or squirrel." Top Displayers and managers won mink stoles and jackets as sales prizes. We gave away mink checkbook covers, jacketed my Bible with the beautiful fur, and distributed mink pencil caps.

What I really meant was not to think materialistically but to re-member that mink is the best. Always aim for the best because God really wants us to have the best. There is a natural abundance that is ours to have if we don't limit it by taking the "little viewpoint."

"Think big. Attempt great things. Believe big and you'll get big results," I would urge our Displayers. "Don't sweat the small stuff."

I was delighted to see the new Home Interiors people accepting this advice. We were not going to make a huge profit the first year but we were not really in the red, either. I decided that we should pay a small dividend on the stock and give bonuses to the home-office staff and managers. I called my accountant and told him.

"You can't do that," he said, almost shouting into the telephone. "Look here, you'd have no reserve whatsoever. Nobody really expects a dividend or a bonus the first year."

"What do you mean, we'd have no reserve?" I said. "It all depends on what you call reserve. You call it money. I call it people."

In spite of all the dire predictions my accountant made, we paid the dividend and bonuses.

By the end of the year I was feeling pretty pleased with myself. I also realized I was feeling tired. I love to work. Why did I feel as if I couldn't lift a pencil by the end of the day? I decided I had better go to my doctor. Perhaps he might give me some vitamin pills.

I need every ounce of energy I can get to carry me through the second year, I thought. Little did I know just how much strength I was going to need.

Baby Mary. "I was my grandparents' adored child."

This was taken just before Mary
left "Mama and Papa" to live in
Washington State.

Daughter, Ruthie, had many childhood responsibilities around the house, but still had time to care for her beloved puppy. *Below:* Mary's son, Don, learned about work at an early age, and was always able to take things apart and put them back together.

Ralph Shanahan; daughter, Ruth Shanahan; Mary; and son, Don Carter, at a Seminar of Home Interiors in Philadelphia (January 1963)—a dream fulfilled. *Left:* Mary congratulating Christine Hamilton, a winning princess at a Home Interiors Seminar.

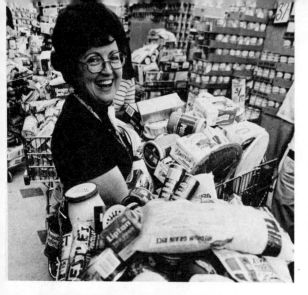

Orena Crabb fills her shopping cart during holiday supermarket spree. *Below:* Mary Crowley with Hugh R. Barbour of Fleming H. Revell Company, Publisher, beside the Falcon Jet "Happy House" (N57HH) Hostessing 1974 Christmas shopping bonanza for employees.

"We started the Don Carter Scholarship Fund to send boys to Fellowship of Christian Athletes conferences." *From left:* Don Carter, John Niland, Mary, and Roger Staubach. *Photo by Bob Kornegay. Below:* Here is the author meeting new displayers and making each person feel important at one of the Home Interiors Rallies. *Photo by Bob Kornegay.*

Announcement of plans for the Mary C Building. *Standing, left to right:* Pearl Burns, Joey Carter (grandson), Linda Carter (daughter-in-law), Don Carter (son), Mrs. W. A. Criswell, Mary Crowley, Dr. W.A. Criswell, Ruth Shanahan (daughter), Ralph Shanahan (son-in-law). *Front row:* Christi Carter (granddaughter), David Shanahan (grandson), and Ronny Carter (grandson). *Photo by Bob Kornegay.* *Below:* Dr. W.A. Criswell dedicates Mary C Building—part of the First Baptist Church complex in Dallas, Texas. *Photo by Bob Kornegay.*

"I presented Salesman of the Decade Award to Billy Graham at Lubbock (Texas) Crusade, 1975." *From left:* Mr. and Mrs. Richard DeVos, Billy Graham, and Mary Crowley. *Photo by Russ Busby.* *Below:* Mary Crowley with singer Ethel Waters—one of the "spiritual giants." *Photo by Bob Kornegay.*

The Church in Our House with Dr. W.A. Criswell—in December, after moving into the new home. "I promised the Lord if I could have this home, it would be used for Him, and He is really using it!" *Photo by Bob Kornegay. Left:* Branch Manager Barbara Fanara in Mary's backyard chapel with a group of displayers on Dallas Displayers Day in October 1975. *Photo by Bob Kornegay.*

A moment of relaxation with son, Don, and daughter, Ruth, at the
1976 Seminar. *Below:* At the Billy Graham Team Retreat in Florida,
January 1976. *From left:* Cliff Barrows, Mary, Corrie ten Boom, and
Billie Barrows. *Photo by Russ Busby.*

Dave and Mary Crowley at home. "He tells me every day that he loves me. That's really what it's all about!" *Photo by Bob Kornegay. Below:* Mary Crowley—"God keeps His promises far beyond anything we could ever imagine."

9
When the Going Is Rough

When I walked into the waiting room at the cobalt-treatment center one morning, I was glad that I had worn my bright pink dress with the polka-dot scarf. Half a dozen people sat around resting their waxy faces in trembling hands, closing their eyes against the light. Worried relatives tried to hide their concern behind newspapers. That hospital smell of anesthesia and disinfectant almost overpowered me.

I picked up a magazine to read but couldn't concentrate on it. Peeking over the cover I saw a motherly looking woman in a bulging gray shirtwaist dress sitting opposite me. She was the type who should have been bustling around a busy kitchen feeding at least a dozen people. Instead she was staring at the floor. From time to time she pressed a tissue against her red eyes.

I couldn't stand it any longer. I walked over and sat down beside her on the sofa.

"Oh, honey, can I be of help?" I asked. The woman wadded up her tissue into a little ball and rolled it between her hands.

"No, nobody can help," she said. "I've got to go in there." She pointed to the door that said TREATMENT ROOM.

"You're going to take cobalt treatments?" I asked. When I said that, the tears simply rolled down her cheeks and plopped onto her gray dress. She nodded.

"I'm so scared," she managed to gasp. "All that pain. . . ."

"Why, honey, cobalt treatments don't hurt," I said. "You don't feel a thing. They may make you a little sick afterward, but they really don't hurt." She dabbed at her eyes with the little wad of tissue.

"They don't?" she said. "Then why didn't my doctor tell me?"

"I don't know," I said. "He should have. Maybe he just thought you'd know." Now she was eyeing me suspiciously.

"How would you know they don't hurt?" she began. At that moment, the nurse opened the glass window and called my name.

"I've got to go now. It's my turn," I said. The woman stared at my pink dress, the gay little scarf, and my smile.

"You mean, you take cobalt treatments, too?"

"Sure I do," I said. "And remember, they don't hurt. They will make you well."

Somehow, even though I was to be nauseated after that cobalt treatment as usual, I felt better that day for having helped that woman. As for myself, I always knew that I was going to get well. Even when the doctor had diagnosed my "fatigue" as a malignancy, even after I underwent radium implants and cobalt treatments, I knew I was going to get well.

The Bible verse I claimed was: "Being confident of this very thing, that he which hath begun a good work in you will perform it until the day of Jesus Christ" (Philippians 1:6). Had not God begun a wonderful, mighty work in Home Interiors and Gifts only a year before? Wasn't I really needed to bring the dreams to fruition? God would heal this illness: I had the best doctors and they had assured me the cancer had been caught early—which is very important in healing.

I won't say that I was not concerned. My family and friends were plenty scared. But when I prayed to be cured, I never expected not to get well. Often I found myself praying, "Lord, give me patience. Let me be Christian and a good patient and not be depressed. Let me be somebody You'll be proud of through this experience."

It is when the going is rough that we are truly tested as Christians. I wanted to be positive and optimistic throughout my illness. I always dressed up and tried to look my most cheerful when I went for cobalt.

My wonderful doctor, Dr. John Mallams, really understood me.

"I can't afford to stay home from work sick," I protested. He only smiled a moment.

"I know how you lady executives are. I couldn't keep you from going to work if I tried," he said. "You may spend two hours a day at the office."

I thanked him, never realizing what a master psychologist he was. As head of the Baylor Hospital Cancer Division, he well knew the cobalt treatments would make me so weak and sometimes ill that I wouldn't be able to work very long at my desk. But this fabulous, effervescent young doctor understood that I could accept the limitation better if it were my decision, not his.

All during the early part of 1959, when I wanted to be training, recruiting, and holding Home Interiors shows myself, my wonderful "people reserve" carried through. We didn't shatter any performance records but we did continue to function.

As for myself, a platform of prayer supported me. I could literally feel the Home Interiors people, my Sunday-school class members, church friends and many, many others praying for me. Not all of them told me of their prayers. But I could feel some great power that I knew was not myself comforting me and removing my anxiety. I can only attribute this feeling to their prayers.

After the cobalt treatments I was able to return to work. My only problem was that I still felt tired. When my strength gave out, I just had to quit whatever I was doing, even if I was crossing a street, and go to bed. This fatigue was more of a trial to me than the thought of having cancer.

With the company's operation back in my hands, Don decided that he would go back to college and finish his degree. Don had been going through a lonely period in his life. While in the air force, he had married. A baby girl was born, without a left hip joint, and the trauma that had followed ended the marriage in divorce. Now he had met and married a wonderful, loving girl named Linda. Ruthie, meanwhile, had married a talented young man named Ralph Shanahan, who had a master's degree from Texas A.&M. When Ralph went to work for Bell Telephone Laboratories in New Jersey, he continued his studies to earn a Ph.D. and Ruthie opened up the East Coast for Home Interiors.

I used to train Displayers in leadership by pointing out that you can lead a horse to water, but you can't make him drink. "But you can feed him salt and make him thirsty—and he will beat you to the trough." Ruthie simplified that statement to "You can't lead a horse from behind." (By now, of course, we had begun to call this gracious, mature daughter "Ruth.")

By 1962, the Home Interiors sales team recorded one million dollars in sales for the first year. After finishing college and working with IBM as the youngest customer-service engineer, Don returned to help build Home Interiors. He already knew the warehousing end of the business. Now he began to deal with suppliers and to learn the merchandising and financial end. He has been a tremendous asset and a dynamic force in our unusual financial growth ever since.

The year 1963 looked as though it would be another winner, too, until November 22. That was the day that President John F. Kennedy was assassinated. We were as shocked as everyone else in the nation, and especially saddened that the tragedy had happened in Dallas. We were even more dismayed to read in the newspapers that all over the nation Americans were blaming our city.

Then, out of the blue, the guests at a Home Interiors show in Pennsylvania canceled their orders. They were having nothing to do with a company headquartered in Dallas. Some Displayers resigned. The shock and depression all over the nation brought the Christmas season to a standstill.

We had Christmas merchandise tied up in customs in New Orleans and Houston. That year we had so much stock left over that it had to sit in the warehouse for many months. With our money tied up in merchandise, we had only enough profit to pay our bonuses and dividends. We have had our share of tough years, and 1963 was one of them.

"What can we do to encourage our sales staff when circumstances beyond our control take over?" I asked Don one morning. Don shook his head.

"People are just reacting to the shock and horror," he said. "The important thing is to make our people realize they shouldn't take anything that is said personally."

"The trouble is," I said, "we're used to push-button living and instant coffee, tea, and potatoes. Jesus said the mountain would move if we believed. He didn't say it would happen *instantaneously.*"

"But how are we going to demonstrate our faith?" Don asked. It was a good question. I thought of that old depression saying "There ain't much business did no more that ain't went out after." For the first time we offered double hostess merits during the entire month of January. The hostesses received double the amount of gifts. And the Displayers worked twice as hard to serve them. They made more money than ever and regained their optimism. We learned management strategy that was to help out during other bad times.

Fear can paralyze. It must be overcome. The greatest news of all time was introduced by *"Fear not,* I bring you tidings of great joy" (*see* Luke 2:10, author's italics). Even the shepherds had to lose their fear before they could hear God's Good News. God does take care of us but He expects us to *believe* in His goodness and promises and act accordingly—Seneca said, a long time ago, "A person really believes something when he acts as if it were so."

During 1974, another year when a recession made the going rough, I spoke at seminars on how to make your dreams come true in spite of difficulties.

"Begin with the dream," I shared with our Displayers and managers. "See yourself as an achiever, a queen. Reject the fact that you're handicapped in any way. Imagine yourself as a co-worker with God." There is magic in belief, but 90 percent of all people utilize this magic the wrong way by believing in the bad things that can happen— instead of imagining and expecting great things to happen.

I love the Oral Roberts theme song:

Something good is going to happen to you—this very day!

Expect great things to happen to you and work to bring them about.

It is not enough to want. You must want *to*—you must want to *do* and to *be* somebody. Ten two-letter words can change your life: *If it is to be, it is up to me.*

So be daring. A lot of people sit back and wait for something good to happen to them and wonder why it never does. Many women hesitate to make decisions, but half of getting anything done is taking the first step.

A lot of people believe it is better to set their goals low so that they won't fail. I say, set your goals high and fail if you have to. *Daring* generates *excitement, excitement* generates *enthusiasm,* and *enthusiasm* generates *energy.* The priceless gift of self-confidence must come from within.

Don't forget to affirm your success. Boldly predict you're going to do something and then be persistent. Stay with it. You may give out but never give up.

Accept the things you can't change and change the things you can. But remember, often the roads that look like terminals turn out to be *tunnels* to new opportunity. Just don't try to do everything all by yourself, but remember Psalm 37—my "pattern for living"—and "Commit everything to Him and He will bring it to pass" (*see* verse 5). Once you become partners with God, expect great things to happen. I am learning to say, with Paul, "I can do *all* things through Christ which strengtheneth me" (Philippians 4:13, author's italics). In Him—not in myself; by surrender and abiding in Him, I am strengthened as a person—all my powers are heightened; a *plus* is added to everything—a divine *plus* that heightens my abilities—my capabilities —my energies—O the joy of knowing that though I slip—God does not fall—and little is much when God is in it!

I have another slogan on my desk: "Attempt something so great that it is bound to fail unless God is in it."

God is so good—so good to me.

O that I might be more like Him every day—more giving—and forgiving—more caring—and forbearing. I have learned that you truly can't *outgive God*—but that if I only give to receive, I am merely swapping—not giving.

I read some lines somewhere, sometime, that exhorted me to be a "spendthrift in love": "Give it away, throw it away, splash it over, empty your pockets, shake the basket, turn the glass upside down— and tomorrow you shall have more than ever." I found it to be great advice—I practiced it and loved doing it.

I dreamed and expected to be a success and I learned to turn my troubles (well, most of them) over to the Lord. My Real Boss is never out!

Truly God has blessed me through Home Interiors, and He has used Home Interiors as a channel for His love and blessings to others. We like to think we are God's pipeline. I know why God blesses Christians. He does it so that we might be enabled to give to His work and share with other people. I don't know why He blesses non-Christians. That's their problem. But it is a thrill to me to watch the lives of countless women—and men, too—being blessed because Home Interiors is dedicated to the Lord.

You only have to know the amazing story of Pearl Burns and Frances Podboreski to see God's blessings in action.

10
Lives That Have Been Touched

Every year I receive hundreds of letters from women who tell me that their careers with Home Interiors have made them feel better about themselves as persons. They have become better wives and mothers. Every year they seem to get younger instead of older. These women look radiant because they are helping others live happier, more effective lives. They make a contribution to their homes, their families, and their communities.

The case of Pearl Burns, our Eastern Area Manager, and Frances Podboreski, a Displayer who was one of Pearl's first recruits, is an outstanding example of Home Interiors' love and fulfillment.

Frances had undergone surgery so many times during her life she had almost lost count. Her medical problems were many. In fact, when she had started as a Displayer ten years earlier, she had told Pearl her career might be limited. Already she limped badly on a built-up shoe—and the doctors were gloomily predicting life in a wheelchair and so on.

Then Frances, who lives in Bangor, Pennsylvania, visited a very busy surgeon with a waiting list in Philadelphia who promised a radical new operation that might help.

Right before Thanksgiving, Frances received a call from the hospital. The doctor would operate if she could check into the hospital the next day.

"I can't go now," Frances told Pearl. "This is the holiday season. It's the busiest time of the year for Home Interiors."

"Don't worry—the whole unit will help," Pearl said.

But Frances looked disheartened. "There'll be weeks and weeks of convalescence . . . all that pain." Her lip tightened. "I won't go. After all, I won't die if I don't have the operation."

"Now, Frances, you've just got to get that surgery," Pearl said. "It's the only thing that will help." Right away Pearl began packing Frances's suitcase and helping her make plans for the hour-and-a-half trip to Philadelphia and the long convalescence. She would be glad she had done so.

That night, Pearl took time to pray. "Lord, Frances just has to have something to reach out for, but I don't know what it is. Tell me." The answer came as clearly as if the Lord were in the room.

"It's the trip," He said. "Frances has always wanted to go to Italy."

Pearl knew that her area's production would be high enough to qualify her for a Home Interiors trip to Europe. She had never traveled there herself. But she didn't hesitate. She tucked something extra into Frances's suitcase.

The next day she drove Frances to Philadelphia, checked her into a gray hospital room with mildewed drapes, and tried to cheer her as a young nurse started puncturing her arm with needles.

"I just wish I hadn't come," Frances was saying. But suddenly Pearl unfurled a big poster of Italy and taped it to the dingy wall.

"Oh, you mustn't put anything on the wall," the nurse said.

"Oh, yes, we must," Pearl said. "This lady is going to Italy and she needs this poster to remind her." Frances stared.

"What are you talking about, Pearl?" Frances asked. "The only place I'm going is to the operating room."

"I'm talking about Italy, Frances," Pearl said. "You're going on my trip. The Lord has directed me, and that's the way it's going to be."

For weeks after the operation, Frances lay in pain in that dismal hospital room. Every time she looked at the poster on the wall, she thought of the love of Pearl. And she did go to Italy. She walked all over Rome. Years before, in 1961, her first full year as a Displayer, Frances had become Home Interiors' First National Queen of Displayers.

We at Home Interiors love Frances, not only because of her determination to overcome handicaps but also because she shares her faith and love with others. She consistently does a great job.

We love Pearl Burns, too. I have a special place in my heart for her because Pearl was trained by my daughter, Ruth, when she and Ralph moved to New Jersey.

Pearl had heard about Home Interiors through her sister in Washington, D.C., who had written the Dallas office asking how Pearl might become a Displayer. I looked on the map and saw that Pearl's hometown was only "half an inch" from where Ruth lived. I wrote, suggesting she drive over to see Ruth.

I did not realize that the one-half inch on the map represented seventy miles of crowded highways. But without hesitation, Pearl jumped into her car and went to visit Ruth. She felt something special in Ruth that she wanted in her life—and she joined Home Interiors. In no time at all she had worked her way up from new Displayer to unit manager, then branch manager, and finally Eastern Area Manager.

Pearl tells me that she came to Home Interiors as a nominal Christian. Now she has found the Lord as a very personal friend. (In fact, it was while attending the funeral service for our friend Ralph Baker that Pearl made a personal commitment to the Lord.)

Mary Dennis, one of our mature Displayers who was crowned National Queen of Displayers for 1974, is a hard worker who speaks with a trace of Old World accent. Once she wrote a letter that thrilled me.

"God used to be just a Sunday outing," she wrote. "Through your influence and my work with Home Interiors, He is now my constant companion."

Husbands notice the difference when their wives start working as Displayers, too.

"My husband even whistles at me again," wrote one.

Another young husband once attended a seminar meeting with his wife. He did not come willingly. He just didn't understand what his wife got out of those Monday-morning sales meetings. He couldn't believe it when she returned from rallies with almost the same glow she had had the day she wore her wedding gown.

And now she was insisting that he attend the seminar where she would be presented an award. The husband grew more and more irritated on the long trip. To make things worse, their car broke down. But after the seminar, he wrote me this letter:

> I am a high-school coach. My whole life is spent motivating young athletes to achieve. Of all people, I should have been able to understand what an organization such as Home Interiors could mean to a woman, but I didn't. Only when I saw the joy and utter fulfillment on my wife's face as she walked down the runway to receive her prize did I realize what winning could mean to her. I want to thank you for helping me see that wives need trophies, too.

Children see their Home Interiors mothers in a new light, too. Barbara Hammond, Western Area Manager and now National Assistant Sales Manager, says that her natural shyness just bloomed into confidence as she advanced in the company. Early in her career with the company, she received a Queen of Displayers crown and a mink stole. But the greatest honor she won she found at her closet door.

One day she came home to find a whole line of little boys at her front door. "Richie, what on earth is going on here?" she called to her twelve-year-old. She found Richie at her closet door, surrounded by more boys.

"I told them you won a mink coat," Richie said. "But they wouldn't believe it unless they saw it. Now they want to feel it, too."

Home Interiors children see their mothers as important people, being paid in direct relation to their ability and dedication. They are proud of their mothers in special ways. They grow up understanding how free enterprise works better than if they studied it in a book.

Home Interiors does not take women out of the home. It keeps them in the home and teaches them to make their homes very important. A woman who does not want to work full time can remain a Displayer all her life if she wishes. She can schedule shows at times that are best for the family.

Managers work full time, but a spare room in their homes most often serves as their office and conference room.

When I started Home Interiors, I mainly tried to recruit women with children of school age or older. I thought mothers of preschoolers should stay at home and take care of them. Then I went into a lot of homes where shows were being held. I saw that some mothers were just plain bored with taking care of children all day.

A lot of women, I realized, were trying to coffee and soap-opera their boredom away. The more they tried this escape, the unhappier they became. Little problems grew like fertilized weeds. Soon the friction between wife, husband, and children would become unbearable.

I realized that a lot of mothers would be more effective if they could get out of the house for a while. They needed the stimulation, the feeling of creativity that they could get by working part time.

Besides that, a lot of young mothers have no cash at all that they can call their own. A little money for going to the beauty parlor or buying a new dress can work wonders in faltering marriages.

So we now recruit young mothers, too. We tell them that time spent with their families is a quality, not a quantity. We have a welcoming tape that is sent to each new Displayer. In it, I tell her, "You are now in business—in fact, you have two businesses—one for love, your family—and one for fun and profit, your Home Interiors business—and we want to teach you to so manage your time and energy and attention that neither goes bankrupt. You can no longer afford to coffee the morning away. Time is money and life."

Amazingly, most manage to do just as much housework as if they had been at home all day. The children, the husbands, and the women are all a lot happier.

One of the top Displayers in the nation one year was Polly Gentry. This attractive mother of twelve gave birth to her thirteenth child in December of the same year. Don't ask me how she multiplies her time. I only know that God can work miracles with hours dedicated to Him.

Another Displayer wrote, "The most important thing I've received from Home Interiors is training that enables us to create inspiration in others. The Home Interiors Way can be applied to everything we do in life. The best part is it always works."

One reason women are happier working for Home Interiors is that they are automatically included in a warm circle of fellowship. Units meet every Monday morning for sales training, recognition, and inspiration. Home Interiors managers and Displayers really care about each other.

One manager with a normally terminal disease (unless a miracle cure is found) has been corresponding with the son of a Displayer in another state. This boy was so severely burned in an accident that he almost died. Our manager writes to him often "to share the pain." Her hope for him helps her to live through her own trauma and pain, and her courage inspires all our people as we make a circle of prayer around the nation.

It has been said of America that today most people lack the "extended family" of grandparents, uncles, aunts, and cousins who live nearby and can help in time of trouble. Home Interiors "sisters" have served each other in just that way. I know what this "extended family" meant to me following my own daughter's tragedy back in 1960.

After seven years of marriage, Ruth's first baby was born. I flew to New Jersey to see him. Ralph and I peered through the hospital nursery and bubbled over with pride when we saw his plump little body and tiny, strong fists.

"He is just so dear and perfect!" I told Ralph. We both thanked the Lord for bringing him safely into the world.

I had planned to attend a rally in New Jersey which was scheduled for the very next day. But by the evening, the doctor told us the baby was having difficulty breathing and was running a high temperature.

"It seems to be a staph infection," the doctor told us in Ruthie's room.

"Isn't that pretty dangerous?" I asked.

"Try not to worry," the doctor said. "We think we can lick this thing. He'll get the best of care."

Ralph, Ruth, and I all prayed for the baby through a fitful night. The next morning Ralph went by the hospital early. Peering through the glass he could see his dear little son, his chest moving up and down regularly with the help of a respirator. When I called Ruth's room, the pediatrician was there.

"His condition looks good this morning," he reassured us.

"Well, I don't think I'd better go to the rally," I told Ruth. "I'd rather stay with you."

"Now, Mother," Ruth said. "The doctor says he is all right. You must go to the rally. They need you there, too."

I drove the ninety miles to the rally to spend a busy day. It was late afternoon when I drove up to Ralph and Ruth's house. Ralph came out on the porch to meet me. Something about the way he walked sent a chill down my spine. He ran to me, threw his arms around me, and began to sob. I knew immediately the baby had been taken from us.

"Does Ruthie know?" I managed to ask. Ralph nodded.

"She wouldn't let me call you," he said. "She just kept saying, 'Some of those people have driven a long way to hear my mother. I will be all right. They need her help more than I do.'"

I could not help but be proud that my daughter, in the midst of her grief, had thought of others before herself. And we both learned, firsthand, of the healing that comes through the prayers, visits, and sympathy of a Home Interiors extended family.

Ruth and Ralph soon had another baby, David, who was born in October 1962. And soon Don and Linda had a fine family of three—Joey, born in October 1960; Ronnie, born in March 1962; and a beautiful little redheaded girl, Christi, born in December 1963. I have a total of five beautiful grandchildren, including my eldest granddaughter, Jeanine, Don's daughter by his previous marriage. All of them are very much a part of the Home Interiors family because the business is so much a part of our personal lives.

We are continuously amazed to learn of the miracles that have occurred in the lives of the women who work with Home Interiors. Many learned to "be somebody" by climbing a very real mountain in Colorado.

11
Atop the Mountain

"How do you motivate a Displayer to go out and line up appointments when she is so lacking in self-confidence she is afraid people will say no?" asked Pat. This blonde with the pixie eyes dressed in a cozy blue robe in front of the fireplace at "Mary's Mountain Lodge" in Colorado just became a manager six weeks ago. She certainly has the potential to lead other women but she needs help in motivating them to do their best.

I bring every new manager to a five-day retreat in the mountains to train her, to get to know her better, and to let her get to know me and our Home Interiors philosophy. In the evenings, we lounge around a crackling fire nibbling on fruit. I have decorated my mountain den with plaques such as the six-foot-long one over the bookcase that says, "Love One Another," pictures of the beautiful mountains nearby, and my favorite American eagle over the stone fireplace.

This is a good place to share ideas, to learn to solve the problems in our business and in our homes, and to become more fulfilled women.

I like to work with women. I think they're really special. But women do need guidance in leadership. What to do about self-confidence is a question that comes up in every group of new managers I bring to the mountain.

Because the lack of self-confidence is a problem the majority of women face, I have dedicated a great portion of my time to *instilling* confidence in women. I believe in women. I believe in the *dignity* and *importance* of women! And I believe a woman's self-worth is tied up in the character of *God*.

Two years ago we used the book *MS Means Myself* by Gladys Hunt as a textbook for Managers' Convention. I have some additional copies for all new managers.

"We make our own prisons. *God's Invitation is to come out,*" this book says. Knowing some restless, seeking woman who is ill at ease with herself and her world, I have often thought, "She needs to sit on *God's* lap and let Him love and quiet her a bit."

My reply to Pat is, "One of the reasons we hold our Confidence Classes is to instill confidence in each new Displayer—confidence in our plan, confidence in training, confidence in herself. But it is an everlasting job."

Barbara Hammond, my Western Area Manager and recently elected National Assistant Sales Manager, who helps at most of the retreats, says, "But first we must be one thousand percent *sure* we love this business—that we love people, love to help and serve others." Always one of the other area managers—Pearl Burns, Fern Gomez, Nancy Good, or Nita Barker—comes and assists me at the mountain. They are all well-trained, dedicated, executive women.

Now Muriel has a question. She is an older woman with grown children and a young smile.

"But what if two women in your unit are really at odds with each other? What if they're getting all the other women to choose sides?" she asks.

"All right, managers, what would you do?" I ask the group.

"Don't try to handle it over the telephone," says Betty, a black manager. "Get them together in person and talk it out. And don't think the problem will just go away. Problems not faced do not go away, as you say; they go underground."

"That's right," I say. "Deal with their emotions first. You might even have to agree with the women that the problem is terrible rather than trying to preach to them. When people are upset, you have to let their emotions come out first. Then they'll most likely work out their own solutions."

Now Pat has another question.

"But I have this one Displayer who just can't deal with negative thinking at a show," she says. "She can't seem to react with anything but dislike and fear."

"You see," I say, "there is so much negative thinking in the news that people absorb it. When they come to a show, they want to be 'lifted up'—inspired and stimulated. We, the Displayers, must be able to do this at a show.

"Remember, we must constantly remind all Displayers and ourselves of *our four loves in this business:*

1. Love of things beautiful (that is, the enjoyment of them, not the things themselves, for things are made to be used and people are made to be loved).

2. Love of people—all kinds, from the sweet to the sour.

3. Love of learning—for we are continually learning in this business.

4. Love of *work,* for this business is work. Everything worthwhile is work.

"Always try to look at every woman through the eyes of love. People who are negative or critical are making a plea for help and attention they can't get any other way. Give them some attention by letting them help with the arrangements you are showing, or let them pass out order forms.

"In fact, some of the best advice you can give every Displayer is to imagine that every person you meet has a sign around her neck which says, PLEASE MAKE ME FEEL IMPORTANT."

Before we go to bed, we will gather around the piano to sing songs such as this one written especially for Home Interiors:

Make your world more beautiful for everyone.
Let your light shine brighter every day.
For you're *someone,* especially to those you love.
And love will always find a way
To make your life a lovely place for all to share.
Make your heart a shelter of God's love.
Make your home a refuge for your family,
A place of happiness for everyone.

When all eighteen of us gather together, join hands, and sing "Kum-ba-yah" (our evening prayer), God's presence is strong within us. Now we are parting, some of the managers going to the three large bedrooms downstairs. Some will sleep upstairs in the bedroom and some in the living room upstairs in front of another massive stone fireplace. This enormous room contains a number of sofas, a huge formal dining table, and an open kitchen with breakfast bar which I keep piled high with fruit and snacks.

The full-length windows that open onto the front porch and back deck are dark now. But in the morning, the sun will polish the golden brass of the mountaintops through those windows, for we are 9,000 feet up on the 14,197-foot Mount Princeton.

Several years ago I was offered the chance to buy property in Lost Creek Ranch, a planned development of summer homes owned by Christian families near Buena Vista, Colorado. Almost on a whim, I bought property as a vacation spot for myself and my family—but upon further thought, decided to build a large lodge on the land— large enough for new-manager retreats.

Later, Home Interiors bought a beautiful, split-level, rustic cabin in a clump of trees nearby. We have had many wonderful family vacations there together. We snowmobile on the roads and meadows. Together we explore mountain trails in a four-wheel-drive Scout. I've been known to drive up deserted ruts in it myself, too. I made it to the top of Mount Princeton, where the view was forever! (Linda and my grandchildren went with me! Bravery runs in the family!)

We've tiptoed past deer, peered out the windows at bear, fed the flag-blue mountain jays, gloried in the aspens which turn shimmering gold in the fall. We've breathed in the crisp Colorado air, and most of all, enjoyed the peace and closeness of God.

Our family has been happy to share these homes with Home Interiors people and friends from all over. The retreats are a wonderful way for me to fellowship with each manager. We have a lot of fun. We explore the little shops that sell geodes, silver Indian jewelry, and souvenirs in nearby Buena Vista. We drive through the mountains to a ghost town. And we study together, too.

Because Proverbs has meant so much to me, I use this book of the

Bible as the best guide for women managers who must motivate other women. We give all our managers a Living Bible bound in leather—with her name on it. I usually remember Bible verses from the King James Version for that is how I memorized them, but we use the Living Bible for study in Proverbs for it is paraphrased in today's language.

"Trust in the Lord with all thine heart; and *lean not unto thine own understanding.* In all thy ways acknowledge him, and *he shall direct thy paths*" (Proverbs 3:5,6, author's italics). Ruthie has needlepointed these verses into a wall hanging for me because she knows they are some of my favorites.

We study Proverbs not as advice passed down thousands of years ago from Solomon to his sons but as rules for living and working with other women today. We seek the promises outlined in Proverbs: "Withhold not good from them to whom it is due, when it is in the power of thine hand to do it" (3:27) is one of these. As managers, these women are in a position to give the praise, recognition, and affirmation that builds others.

"This means, dwell on your Displayers' strong points, not their weaknesses, and they will accomplish far more than you ever expected," I point out. I also like to quote the old Indian proverbs, "If you help someone else row his boat across the lake—you will reach the other shore yourself," and, "Give a man a fish and he eats for a day. Teach him to fish and he eats for a lifetime."

So many women who haven't had the opportunity to go to the mountain have wanted to learn from Proverbs, so I wrote *Women Who Win*. But the best way is to discuss it with other dedicated Christians.

Most women learn easily the rules for successful management. The problem comes in carrying them out. Success is like housework—it is so daily! You have to do it all over again every morning. Remember, you can't rest on your laurels. If you do, they will wilt! There is plenty of room at the top, but no room to sit down.

So how do you choose what is really essential to do each day in the year?

On the back of my calling card I had printed: "Every morning lean thine arm a while upon the window sill of heaven and gaze upon thy God. Then with that vision in thine heart, turn strong to meet the day."

I suggest that each morning you write down five or six things that you know must be done that day. The number-one task is to spend a little time with the Lord before the pressures of the day fall in on you. Remember that God can do more with nine-tenths of your day than you can do alone with all of it. Spend the time praying or reading an inspirational book or the Bible, or in listening to hymns dear to your heart—and sing along with them: "Jesus loves *me!* this I *know.*" That's a glorious, positive thought to start the day. But you have to plan this time before the telephone starts ringing.

After this, set priorities for the other tasks for the day. The priorities may be different from the way you would have rated them before spending time with the Lord.

As you finish a task, cross it off the list. You may always end up with some goals unmet for the day but you will have done the most important ones. Every time you cross off another task, you have consciously eliminated that much stress and strain.

I think the mountaintop experiences of our managers in Colorado definitely filter down through the Home Interiors ranks. Sometimes our seminars and rallies can be a different kind of "mountaintop" experience.

Pat Boone has led the singing and inspirational talks at some of our seminars, Cliff and Billie Barrows at others. I first met the Barrows in 1952 when the Billy Graham Crusade came to Dallas and I was singing in the First Baptist Church choir. I felt Cliff's magnetism then but I didn't really know him personally. Then in 1971 when I led the women's committee in preparing for another crusade, Cliff spoke to us. Since then I have known both Billie and Cliff well.

This wonderful couple has five children and lives in a warm, loving home that is a mixture of Swiss chalet and Country Western. The whole atmosphere is one of beautiful, exciting, happy people. When the Barrows spoke at the 1975 seminars, I felt they were a perfect example of a Christian marriage.

"It's a Happy Day, and I'm Livin' It for My Lord," rang out the voices of the two thousand or so women as Cliff led them in song. Then Billie assured the women that even a marriage that looked as perfect as her own had its share of tensions. Cliff had always had to be away from home a great deal, and she had the responsibility of the five children. "Marriage," she said, "is a union of two good forgivers.

" 'I love you' and 'Please forgive me' and 'I'm sorry' ought to be heard in a home, even by the children," she said.

Then Cliff quoted Proverbs 14:1: "A wise woman builds her house, while a foolish woman tears hers down by her own efforts" (LB).

"Family prayer and the power of the Holy Spirit can help any woman solve her problems both at home and in her business," Cliff pointed out.

As the Home Interiors women poured out of the hotel that day, dressed in smart dresses and suits, I noticed a businessman in the foyer watching us curiously. Finally he could stand it no longer.

"Who are all these women?" he asked me. I told him they were Home Interiors Displayers and managers who were attending a seminar.

"They certainly stand out in a crowd," the man said. "They dress the way women should. They're pretty. *They look enlightened.*"

Home Interiors women look like "somebodies" because they know my mountaintop secret of living: If you work for the things you believe in, you are rich, though the way is rough. If you work only for money, you can never make quite enough.

As for myself, I learned long ago that one of the real reasons for working is to earn money to be able to share it in a creative way—and double the enjoyment.

I once told our young attorney friend, Doug Adkins, that I wanted my will to read: "Being of sound mind I spent—and gave away—every last cent I had."

12
Living Water

"ABC is on the phone," said Peaches Mathews, my assistant and secretary, on the afternoon of the second day of our Christmas grocery-shopping spree in 1974. Peaches, a slender brunette who has two sons in the ministry and the efficiency of a perfectly programmed computer, is usually vivacious but calm. Today she was practically breathless.

"ABC who?" I said, shuffling through some papers on my desk. "I don't know any company by that name."

"No, no, it's not a business call. It's the American Broadcasting Company in Chicago," she said. "And they're in a hurry."

"Why, what would ABC want with me?" I asked.

"I think it must be about the Christmas shopping spree," she said.

The shopping spree had been Don's idea after reading headlines that screamed "unemployment" day after day. People seemed to be able to talk of nothing but the recession. The gloom as we approached Christmas 1974 recalled the dreary holidays of the 1930s.

I really felt the recession was more feeling than fact. If people would just stop being gloomy and take a step in faith, the recession would be gone in a minute.

"If you have let down your bucket into the well and it has come up half-empty, lengthen the rope—don't kick the bucket," I kept saying to my business friends.

But how could we lengthen the rope at Home Interiors among our own employees? How could we calm their fears for themselves and their families? How could we encourage all our people to Think Mink —when all about, people were crying wolf?

We had always had some exciting Christmas parties for the home-office staff because we know that our warehouse-and-office workers miss out on the fun and inspiration of seminars and rallies.

One year we parked several brand-new cars, all tied up in ten-inch-wide red ribbon, in front of the warehouse. Then we held a drawing for one-year leases on them. For the five following years we gave away eight cars a year. We had spent as much as fifty thousand dollars taking employees' children on shopping sprees for clothes and toys. We loved sharing the profits they had helped make.

But in the fall of 1974, we wanted to add something else to disperse the gloom on TV and in the newspapers. Home Interiors had actually experienced a good year. We wanted to overcome any doubts for the future by giving something extra that would fill a need at home.

Then Don came bursting into my office with an idea.

"Besides our regular Christmas party with gifts, cars, bonuses, and toys, what do you think about this? We'll just line everybody up at the supermarket, give them a shopping cart, and ring a starting bell. Then for one whole hour, everybody can load as many groceries as they can pack into their carts. And we'll pay the bill!"

I liked it. Andy Horner liked it. We arranged with two different Safeways to hold our grocery-shopping sprees before the stores opened to the public. On the first morning, the Dallas employees would shop. The next day, the employees at our distribution center in Lewisville, Texas, would do the same thing. The McKinney staff would shop the third day.

"Safeway thinks our shopping spree should make a good story for the Dallas papers," Don told me the day before the event. "They've phoned the food editors of both our Dallas papers."

Meanwhile, we had told our Dallas employees to come to work at 6:30 A.M. one day in December for a special surprise. (We had not told them what the surprise would be. But not a single one showed up late! And no one was absent!)

That morning, as they boarded the chartered buses we had at the warehouse, they saw two empty extra buses.

"Those buses will be loaded with all the groceries you're going to bring back," Don told them. The chattering and laughter all the way to the Safeway told us we had had a great idea—even the mute people who work for us were all smiles as they read the good news!

But at the store we discovered only one of the Dallas newspapers had bothered to send a reporter and photographer. And the reporter was definitely unimpressed.

As everybody lined up with his grocery cart, one woman had tears rolling down her cheeks.

"What's the matter, honey?" I asked her.

"Oh, Mrs. Crowley," she sobbed. "All my life I've wanted to go to a supermarket and put anything I wanted in my cart without looking at the price!" I laughed.

"Honey, that's something I've always wanted to do, too," I said. The reporter just leaned against a counter yawning and looking at her watch.

"I can't believe I'm in a supermarket at 7:30 A.M.," I heard her tell the ruddy-cheeked young photographer. If she was bored, he was not. With three cameras flopping around his neck, he took off with our employees at the starting bell. He snapped photos of smiles, tears, jumping eyebrows, and flying hands as our employees snatched at the most valuable groceries and stacked their carts as high as they could.

Joe Ramos, one of our warehouse men, had been married only a few months. He had never shopped at a supermarket before.

"What should I get, Mrs. Crowley?" he asked, seemingly hypnotized by shelves stacked high with unfamiliar cans, vegetables, and packages.

"What about sugar? It's selling at $2.50 for five pounds," I said.

"Get some salmon—and some canned hams," Don called.

"Get your wife lots of pecans and shortening so she can bake for Christmas," I shouted after him as he took off at a lope.

Roy Jones, a bachelor, rolled his cartful of canned prepared dinners.

"I've got more than I can eat for a year. Now I'm buying things for my grandmother and to share with my church mission program," he said.

At the end of the hour, the checkout clerks looked at those bulging carts and almost groaned. Our best shopper had managed to stuff thirty-two sacks of groceries in his cart.

One young fellow watched his approximately three hundred dollars worth of groceries being tallied.

"Mrs. Crowley, I only became a Christian last Sunday," he said. "My wife said we should pray about not having very much money for food this week, but I didn't know God would answer so quickly and so big!"

"God doesn't always answer so quickly," I smiled, "but He does always supply our needs."

Don and I had never had such a good time in all our lives. But the story in the newspaper was only three inches long; however, there was a great picture taken by the enthusiastic photographer. In the local section of a late edition, the headline read, "Grocery Bill of Dallasite Hits $40,000." It was obvious they didn't think our shopping spree very newsworthy.

But it seems that the wire service had read the tiny story. When I talked to the ABC man in Chicago, he wanted all the details for his 6:00 P.M. radio newscast that evening.

Before I could hang up the phone, Peaches came tiptoeing into my office.

"It's ABC from Atlanta. They want to know the address of the supermarket in McKinney where tomorrow's shopping spree will be held," she whispered. "And they want to know the name of a motel where their camera crew can stay."

"Camera crew?" I said. "Why, I don't know anything about the motels in McKinney." No sooner had I finished talking to ABC when Don walked into my office.

"I just talked to CBS!" he said in awe. "They're going to fly a camera crew into McKinney tomorrow."

"Well, that was ABC on my phone," I said. "They're sending a filming crew here in the morning. What'll we do?" Don just threw back his head and whooped.

"What'll you do? Just let her rip, lady!" he chuckled.

And rip they did. In the McKinney supermarket, our employees tripped over tripods and electrical wires. They kept bumping into cameramen weighted down like camels with their television equipment.

And so the good news and our positive outlook for the future were telecast and reported literally all over the world. My son-in-law, Ralph, called to say we made the *New York Times.* We received clippings from the *London Times* and from newspapers in the Philippines. The *Stars and Stripes* ran the story in its overseas edition and we received copies from Germany and Turkey. The world was simply hungry for the good news that we could supply. Never have we enjoyed spending $71,165 so much!

I really loved the write-up in the Lewisville paper, which had lots of photos and comments from employees. Joan Butler, who had worked with us for five years, said, "I like working for Home Interiors so much they couldn't pay me to quit!"

But the statement that thrilled us most came from an employee who said, "They're Christian people. They don't just say it. They do it. They live by it. It's wonderful to work for them. This is the way the world should be."

A year later, during the week we held our 1975 Christmas shopping sprees, Dr. Leighton Ford telecast this inspirational news feature:

"In case you woke up this morning feeling like a nobody, you could use a little of what makes Mary Crowley tick," he said, describing the Christmas shopping sprees.

"But that's only the beginning of Mary Crowley's sharing program. A committed believer in Jesus Christ and a member of Billy Graham's board, she also believes in sharing her faith.

" 'Be somebody,' she urges readers of her weekly column in a company newsletter. 'God never takes time to make a nobody.

" 'As soon as people know that God loves them and others care, life begins to take on importance and purpose,' she says.

"Today, be a somebody. That begins when you accept the reality of the love of God."

The day after the McKinney Christmas spree, I strolled out into the garden of our new home-office building. With 160,000 square feet, this graceful, arched white building is forty times as big as our first little warehouse. But all the warm, loving qualities that we originally symbolized in our Happy House logo are the same. I only wished that Ralph Baker could have attended the Christmas shopping sprees himself.

One day late in January 1970, Ralph had called me in Portland, Oregon, where I was attending a seminar.

"I've been out to see the property you and Don talked about for your new headquarters," he said. "It's just the place! I think you ought to buy it right away."

"That's wonderful, Ralph," I said. "Don is in Dallas. You two get together and work it out."

That was my very last conversation with the man who had done so much to influence Home Interiors. The very next day, Ralph was called home—in the middle of a step.

Don and I grieved. My area managers grieved. We were all saddened to lose the man who had guided us so tenderly and lovingly throughout the years that we had been able to transcend even our original intentions.

At first we had seen the company as a way to make a good living for ourselves and for other women. Then we had seen it as a way of helping others. Now we saw it as a means of growing and thriving—in order to be able to create more jobs, more opportunities, more love and care.

Ralph had encouraged us to have swelled hearts, not swelled heads. He had counseled us to put in a marvelous profit-sharing plan which is second to none and already a blessing to many. He had applauded our company's leadership in making a Christian witness.

Now God had taken this wonderful leader, loving husband, and father to Himself. I found it difficult to accept this grief. Why had God called home such a glorious Christian? I do not think it is wrong to ask God why. A precious friend, Hannah Till, once told me she thought it was not wrong to ask why when grief comes our way—provided we ask why when good things come our way. Moments like these can deepen our faith and give us the inspiration to make God's will more meaningful in our own lives—and to lean on Him.

Determined to create a memorial to Ralph in our new building, we drew up plans for an interior garden planted with red azaleas, blooming Carolina jasmine, and trees. A walkway would lead to a fountain gurgling under the open skies. At the foot of the fountain, carved in marble, would be the Holy Bible opened to John 4:13,14.

Whosoever drinketh of this water shall thirst again: But whosoever drinketh of the water that I shall give him shall never thirst; but the water that I shall give him shall be in him a well of water springing up into everlasting life.

The day after the last shopping spree was over, I stood in an unseasonably warm December sunshine, rereading those words at the fountain.

Ralph would have been so proud to know that by 1974 we had 15,000 women serving as Displayers and 350 managers; and that we were selling and serving over $100 million at retail in home accessories. He would have been even prouder to know that in 1973 I had won the Direct Selling Association's Knight of the Royal Way Award. This honor is a recognition of a single direct-selling executive for outstanding humanitarian service and special concern for his fellowman.

The certificate I had received cited Home Interiors' policies in helping Vietnam veterans, the handicapped, and the delinquent, plus the work we had done in spreading the words of the Gospel through the Billy Graham Evangelistic Association.

Ralph would have called all that our "living water."

As for what we did with the handicapped, the federal government called it "impossible." But we knew better.

13
To Find Yourself

It was raining the morning Don and I took the man from Washington to visit the Handi-Hands plant, but there was no gloom anywhere. Some of the employees walked on crutches, others sat in wheelchairs or wore braces. But all of them smiled when they saw us watching them stuff plastic bags with the artificial fruit that goes into our Home Interiors centerpieces, or run the printing press that puts out our weekly newsletter.

"It must cost you a bundle to supplement this operation," the Department of Labor man said as he pulled out a notebook to take down the statistics.

"No, no, we don't supplement it at all," said Don. The man almost dropped his notebook.

"What do you mean, you don't supplement it?"

"Handi-Hands is a separate company owned by these people here. It's their business, not ours."

"Oh, but surely you paid for the building. All these ramps and rest rooms with wide doors for the wheelchairs. That cost something to build."

"Yes, it did," Don said. "And we got them started. But now they bear their own expenses, make a profit, and pay themselves salaries." The man from Washington whistled.

"I didn't think this kind of thing could be done with the handicapped," he said. I laughed.

"But you see," I said, "we never think of the handicapped as being handicapped."

Then we had to tell him how Handi-Hands was born. Don had been hiring minority employees for our warehouse with success long before the government ever heard of Affirmative Action. Then one morning about fourteen years ago, he heard the Caruth Rehabilitation Center urging companies to hire the deaf. "Wouldn't this be another way Home Interiors could help people?" Don asked himself—for Don had always had a special place in his heart for the wounded and the handicapped.

The deaf-mute he hired turned out to be a good, steady worker. Soon he hired another, and another. Now there are about twenty-seven of them. Some have been with us for thirteen years, participate in our profit-sharing program, and can look forward to a secure retirement as well.

They more than make up for their inability to speak or hear by their eagerness to please. Besides, many can read lips. Don has learned their sign language and he carries on conversations with them—kids them and builds their confidence. As for me, I find a big smile and a pat on the back can go a long way toward communicating.

The fact that we would hire the deaf spread like a tidal wave through the handicapped community. Soon badly crippled job hunters were rolling their wheelchairs to Don's office. Professionals who helped the handicapped kept calling us.

"We've got to help those people," Don said. "But they've got to *earn* the money if they are to gain self-respect. We can't just give it to them." Fortunately, we have a lot of hand-packaging and printing to do. We offered these jobs and they took them.

By 1970 we had seventy-five crippled or deaf workers. The American Legion, the Texas Employment Commission, and the United States Department of Labor presented Home Interiors with a special citation for employing the handicapped. In fact, about 20 percent of the home-office and warehouse staff was handicapped. One warehouseman had lost both feet in Vietnam. Vernon Denman, who accepted the award for us, was a double-paraplegic veteran.

Soon afterward, we helped our handicapped workers form their own company, called Handi-Hands. As a separate company, they would contract to receive from us a set amount for each finished package or printing assignment. Out of the money received, the handicapped workers ran their own business.

After our Spring Valley home office was built, Handi-Hands moved into its own small building nearby. Now these workers do not have to compete with the fast pace of our warehouse. They run their business at their own pace—at a profit.

"God doesn't take time to make a nobody," I mused as I looked out over our deaf people packing orders. Don likes to say, "A man is at his tallest when he stoops to help another." I guess that's how Home Interiors got involved with helping the Paul Anderson Youth Homes, too.

One day Don's friend and our attorney, Doug Adkins, told him about Paul Anderson, the Olympic gold medalist who is billed as the "World's Strongest Man." Paul and his wife, Glenda, opened a youth home in 1961 in Vidalia, Georgia, to help teenage boys who had gotten into trouble with the law.

"If it weren't for the Paul Anderson Home, these boys would be placed in a penal institution," Doug told Don. "It costs about sixty-five hundred dollars a year to keep a boy at the home, and it would cost the state thirteen thousand dollars a year to keep him in a penal institution. But the Paul Anderson Home rehabilitates the kids, too. There's only been one boy out of three hundred who ever got into trouble again with the law after living with the Andersons during the past eleven years."

"Sounds as though it's a great program," Don whistled. "What a record!"

"Yes, and now Anderson wants to open another home in Texas," Doug said. "He has a man to take charge. All he needs is a big place out in the country to raise those boys."

Once again, Don and I felt, the Lord had moved in mysterious ways. Don is always looking for ways to invest our profit-sharing money. Only the year before, he had bought the old Wiley Dude Ranch near Lewisville, Texas. This once-elegant vacation spot for city "dudes" had rustic cabins, a big lodge, a swimming pool, and stables. The buildings were a bit run-down now, but the location of the property, near the Dallas-Fort Worth Metroplex, was sure to increase in value. One day Don came into my office with a proposition.

"Why couldn't Paul Anderson use the dude ranch for a Texas youth home? We could work it out so that he could use the property as a trust for as long as he likes," he said.

"Good idea," I agreed. By 1973, Paul's staff had moved in and refurbished the old buildings. The first boys arrived.

But the Lord wasn't going to let us leave it at that. As we visited the home we saw those boys learning to accept responsibility and love. We watched them repair buildings, feed the livestock, do their own ironing.

"My boys don't think the world owes them a living. They are pitching in and doing their share and they can see the results," said Paul, the man who can lift a piano or a small car and now was lifting up boys. Many, in fact, learn to accept the Lord while they are with Paul. As Don and Linda invited the boys to their home or Home Interiors took them on shopping sprees, we could see the boys changing before our eyes.

Naturally, we couldn't help but get involved in the financial support of the home. Soon our Home Interiors women wanted to help, too. Don started auctioning off Home Interiors accessories samples to the highest bidder at every rally or seminar, with the proceeds going to the home. How he learned to auctioneer the way a professional does, I'll never know, but he does it. He must get the message across, too —for he can get these dear gals to pay three hundred dollars for an accessory that they know will retail for thirty or forty dollars.

One Christmas a Home Interiors manager and her husband bought and wrapped and put names on gifts for each of the fourteen boys then at the home. And when Displayers come to Dallas, the Anderson Youth Home is number one on their requests of places to visit. Checks come in frequently from our people for the home. I find people love to identify with a purpose, a feeling of belonging to and contributing to something worthwhile.

Another wonderful group with which we identify is the Fellowship of Christian Athletes. At its annual conference in Estes Park, Colorado, this national organization gives junior-high and high-school athletes a chance to become acquainted with national sports figures and to hear their Christian witness. Don and his two sons, Joey and Ronnie, had been to Estes Park, Colorado, for a conference in the spring of 1973.

Don had been invited there (yes, urged to go) by big Bill Krisher, an ex-pro football player—now in charge of F.C.A. in the Dallas area —one fantastic Christian guy who had become Don's friend.

Don related his experience well—in his words:

At sunrise, after calisthenics at 6:30 A.M., they have quiet time. The sun at about ten thousand feet is slanting horizontally across that athletic field—and seven hundred and fifty young men are out there—and there is a hush on the hillside—you can hear a pin drop.

The Lord was there—and He taught me an awful lot in a little while. In that few moments the Lord grabbed hold of me and He said, "Carter, if nothing else you have to admit, there are seven hundred and fifty young men—the future leaders of our country —in a reverence that would bring respect from anybody." That opened up my life to the Fellowship of Christian Athletes.

Prior to that I thought it was a fantastic organization that I'd heard about, but that you had to be an all-Pro athlete to be a member—and I never was an athlete. I went to school only half a day in high school—I had to work the other half. I never played any athletics in high school. I never had that opportunity so I thought that wasn't for me—but I found out differently. I found that as a businessman I could have a part in F.C.A. and I could have a part in changing lives. It changed my life—and it changed my outlook—I feel very good about the youth of today.

F.C.A. also prepared me three years later to have a part in changing the direction of a young man's life—a friend of my two sons—in a tremendous way. I thank God for F.C.A.

And I, too, thanked God for F.C.A.—and for Bill Krisher—
and the deepening walk with the Lord they had brought in Don's
life.

Then, the following June, Don and Linda and the family took me
with them to Estes Park for a few days at F.C.A. Conference.

There I saw firsthand what Don had shared—and I, too, felt the
life-changing power on that mountainside. Later, I was talking with
Tom Landry, an active leader in F.C.A., and telling him how im-
pressed I was. "Yes, but I wish more boys could go," Tom said.
"There are a lot of boys who wanted to go to the conference this year,
but they didn't have the money to go."

This gave me an idea: Don's birthday, July 5, was coming up—and
I had been wondering what I could do that would be a gift that he
would enjoy yet would be a continual gift for others.

With the help of Tom Landry, Roger Staubach, and Bill Krisher,
we started the Don Carter Scholarship Fund. Soon our managers
heard of it and they wanted to share in it. Soon there was fifty
thousand dollars in the scholarship fund—enough to send many boys
from all across America to F. C.A. conferences! It continues to grow
and be used for young men—and now young women, too—to have
this life-changing opportunity. By 1979 the scholarship fund had
grown to $100,000. It is in great demand for sending young people to
these wonderful conferences. Don continues to load our company
plane with businessmen and coaches who go to the conferences to
learn about the Fellowship of Christian Athletes.

Last summer my associate teacher in Bible class, Jim Thomas, a
Dallas businessman, and his family went along—the same time I was
there. As we sat in awe of the majestic, snow-capped peaks and in awe
of nine hundred boys and girls listening reverently to the testimony
of famous pro athletes Roger Staubach and Doug Kingswriter, Jim
Thomas turned to me and said, "Just look at those young men. I've
been thinking of the end of the thirties when Hitler took the youth
of Germany into the mountains of Bavaria to turn them into SS
troops. Isn't it glorious that these young men up here in Colorado are
being trained into troops for the Lord."

My heart gets so full at the joy that God has allowed us to have through these glorious experiences—and through the joy of serving and sharing—learning just a little bit more of what He wants us to be.

And what joy we feel when our beautiful Home Interiors people respond so enthusiastically.

The surest way to *find yourself* is to lose yourself in something *bigger than yourself!*

I love God's mathematics: Joy adds and multiplies as you divide it with others, and in laughing, loving, and learning, we have helped countless others to find real joy—and to discern the difference between happiness and joy. *Happiness* comes from the same root word as *happenings:* Happiness so often depends on happenings—atmosphere—environment—others' actions—external things—no one can be happy all the time. A mother cannot be happy if her child is seriously ill. A person cannot be happy with a toothache or a painful ailment. A man can't be happy when he's just lost his job—but one can have *joy*—which comes from the knowledge that God loves me —God cares for me. God has His hand on my life—I am going somewhere, and no matter if the year has been rough—if obstacles loom larger, I can have *joy*—as a sunrise colors the new day!

This is God's gift to the Christian, His special glow to the lives of those who walk and work with Him. This is the "mark" I see on the faces of the great Christians I have been so privileged to know and be with—Christians are pretty exciting people!

And I have been privileged to meet some of the greatest.

14
How God Answers Prayer

"Praise God, from whom all blessings flow," sang the thousands of people at the International Congress on Evangelism at Lausanne, Switzerland, in July 1974. The words seesawed out in Japanese from the couple in front of me, exploded in Dutch from the girl next to me, chimed in French from the man from Zaire behind me.

Nothing has ever sounded more beautiful! I thought. I had come to the congress with Ruth, Ralph, and my grandson, David. I had not expected to go. At first I had simply started raising money to support it. But the more I heard about a worldwide meeting of Christians interested in evangelism, the more determined I became to go myself.

My most precious memory, however, came about because of a side trip we took during the congress to *L'Abri.* This mountain "shelter" *(L'Arbi* means *shelter),* high above the Rhone Valley, is a place where thousands of agnostics, atheists, and confused intellectuals have learned to know God personally through the work of Dr. Francis A. Schaeffer and his wife, Edith.

At *L'Abri* we admired the view of the Alps, visited the chalets where guests study and receive counsel, wondered at the dedication of workers helping cerebral palsied children. And there we met Edith Schaeffer.

"Is it true that the only financial resources for all of this comes from gifts?" someone asked.

"Yes," she said. "We pray that God will send enough money to care for our needs as a family and for food and the expense of those He sends us to help. We feel that both the spiritual and physical food should be freely given."

"Excuse me for asking," said a visitor, "but this is an ideal place for a skiing vacation. Doesn't anybody try to take advantage of you?"

"No, they don't," Edith said. "You see, we also pray that God will send us only the people of His choice. He always hears us."

I had bought all of Francis Schaeffer's books, which I hoped he would autograph. But he was not there. However, a few days later, while lunching in our Lausanne hotel, I spotted both the Schaeffers at an adjoining table.

"I sure would like to get them to autograph my books," I told Ruth and Ralph, "but I would not interrupt their meal." Then the Schaeffers started to leave and I couldn't resist. I walked over to their table. Edith Schaeffer was gracious enough to remember seeing me at *L'Abri,* and Dr. Schaeffer was kind enough to wait for me to go up to my room and get the books. They autographed each one. I read Edith Schaeffer's entire book *L'Abri* on the plane home from Europe, and what an inner lift it gave me. I got a special thrill out of reading the rest of the books after I got home. But then I went into another busy fall of training managers. The Christmas grocery-shopping spree was scheduled for December 10. With all that excitement, I had no time to think about *L'Abri.*

But sometimes, in the middle of a phone call, or while signing a letter, an image of Edith Schaeffer would flit into my mind—the high cost of food was in everyone's mind. Our employees had just received seventy one thousand dollars worth of groceries through the shopping spree. Everyone was talking about food. How were the Schaeffers, who depended entirely on the Holy Spirit to provide gifts, faring in this crisis? *I just must send a check,* I thought.

On Christmas Day this godly couple kept coming to mind, so I sat down in the afternoon and wrote Edith Schaeffer and enclosed a sizable check for food. I mailed the letter the next day.

I was not prepared for the response—and I relate this happening only because we all need encouragement to "Ask—believing—we shall receive" (*see* Mark 11:24).

"How amazing it seemed that with no further contact personally since that summer day in Lausanne, God answered prayer directly!" Edith Schaeffer wrote. "Your gift has met a very present need, but also has come to encourage all the *L'Abri* workers."

She told me how *L'Abri* during the past year had had to cut its meager dinner allotment of $2.50 in Swiss francs (about 82 cents) per person to only $2.00 (about 66 cents). This allotment also covered soaps, cleaning supplies, and broken dishes.

"I have been praying that *before the end of this year,* the Lord would encourage us with a large gift toward the food, that first of all we would be assured that He is hearing and answering as we pray for the material needs, and secondly that in January we could begin the New Year with a full food budget of $2.50 per person per meal," Edith wrote.

She went on to express her astonishment that I had written the letter on Christmas Day, and that the mails, which usually take two weeks, took only five days, arriving December 31 in faraway Switzerland, high on a mountainside in a remote village.

"To see that you had sent such a large gift caused me to know that God was answering prayer on Christmas Day to choose you as the one He would lead to be blended with us in the work He is doing at *L'Abri,* " she wrote. I cannot know why God chose me for this precious experience—but I am thankful.

Yes, the Holy Spirit does nudge us. Often I have fleeting thoughts that I should call a certain Displayer. I don't ignore them. I pick up the phone and call. My Home Interiors women say I have a sixth sense, that I can actually see when they are fearful, doubting, and in need of encouragement. All I can say is that the Holy Spirit does let us know of others' needs. If we help other people get what they want out of life, we will get what we want out of life. As Christians, we are blessed to share our blessings with others.

What wonderful, exciting people I have met by sharing with other Christians! In 1971, I was the only woman to serve on the committee to arrange Billy Graham's Greater Southwest Crusade, to be held in Dallas. This committee was headed by Cowboy Coach Tom Landry. We worked together for a year and a half before the crusade was held.

I was determined that the women's activities would be just as important as the men's. I planned a big rally, to be held two weeks before the crusade, with Ruth Graham as the speaker. The crusade office told me she almost never spoke in public at that time. When she accepted, I was thrilled. I chartered a limousine for her and held a motorcade and a press conference, just as the committee would do for Mr. Graham.

Since then, Ruth and I have enjoyed a close friendship, exchanging frequent correspondence. I like to send Ruth flowers several Monday mornings every month, just to say that I admire and love her.

Ethel Waters also was a speaker at that rally. When she arrived, I reserved a limousine for her, too. I had reserved two identical suites of rooms at a hotel for Ruth and Ethel, and sent baskets of flowers to both suites. But when we walked into Ethel's suite, we found it wasn't a suite—it was one room. I simply picked up the phone and insisted the manager find something better—a suite like the one for Ruth Graham.

I didn't think this was much to do, but Ethel saw it as a big thing. Ever since then, we have continued to correspond. I have come to love her for the dedicated Christian she is.

In 1974, when I was in Los Angeles for a Home Interiors rally, I called Ethel. She was in low spirits. "My eyes are so bad with these cataracts that I can't see to cook for myself," she said. "But that doesn't matter. I'm not hungry anyway."

"Then I'm coming right out to visit you," I said.

"Oh, honey, you can't take time for that. You've got a meeting there with your people," Ethel protested.

"We'll see about that!" I said. I ordered prime ribs with all the fixings from the hotel. Two of my managers drove out with me to her lovely apartment on the eighteenth floor overlooking Los Angeles, and waited two hours for me to visit with Ethel.

Ethel looked so weak and run-down that she could scarcely hold a fork in her hand. As we talked, I helped her eat. I'll never forget that afterward, she went and sat by that window sparkling with lights. That beautiful, high, sweet voice of hers broke out with:

> I'm going to LIVE the way HE wants me to live—
> I'm going to GIVE until there's just no more to give,

I'm going to LOVE—LOVE 'til there's just no more love,
I could never, never outlove the LORD—

This was the first time I had heard the then-new song by Bill and
Gloria Gaither—my heart overflowed with love and joy.

The words of that song still send a thrill up my spine whenever I
hear them—and later, Ethel was to come to Dallas and sing them at
a very special occasion for me—and for my family. How could I ever
thank Him enough for letting me walk with these spiritual giants?

I was to relate this incident later on at the graveside services held
for Ethel Waters. I thought, as I told that story that Ethel truly knew
how to give of self, to share her talent and her faith. God rewarded
her with the abilty to be a great witness for Him, to be instrumental
in leading others to Christ. He blessed her with friends, fame, and
vitality for many years, until at last He was ready to take her to her
eternal home. Her story beautifully illustrates how God can turn even
defeat into victory and blessings and joy for many, when it is committed to Him in faith.

In 1974, I was pleased to learn I had been named the first woman
to serve on the board of directors of the Billy Graham Evangelistic
Association. From this work, I've learned a new appreciation of all
the preparation that goes into a crusade. How God honors preparation and prayer. I've thrilled over the tremendous power of a crusade
to lift people from both spiritual and financial depression. And again,
I've met wonderful, exciting, fulfilled people.

Bill Brown, head of World Wide Pictures, a Billy Graham subsidi-
ary, sent our California managers and me forty tickets to attend the
worldwide premiere of *The Hiding Place,* the tremendous film of
Corrie ten Boom's life. Corrie ten Boom was there, along with all the
stars, Billy and Ruth Graham, the Cliff Barrows, and Pat Boone.
Barbara Hammond and I were so excited to be riding over in the
limousine with Roy and Dale Rogers!

About five minutes before the movie was to begin, while I was
seated in the theater with my managers and their husbands, I heard
a popping noise.

"That sounded like a shot!" I remarked. All of a sudden the people started coughing and I felt a funny feeling in my eyes and throat.

Now we saw people who had been sitting up close to the screen running up the aisle with handkerchiefs pressed against their noses and tears streaming down their faces.

"It's tear gas!" someone gasped. Once outside the theater we were too busy gulping in fresh air to watch the stars being interviewed by television crews. As the crowds milled around coughing, Billy Graham whispered to Pat Boone, "Go get Cliff Barrows to lead some singing!"

"You know, I do a little singing myself, Billy," Pat grinned. While Billy's face turned red, Pat and Cliff found someone with a guitar and a drum. Soon we were all singing some joyous gospel songs in the middle of Wilshire Boulevard in Hollywood, California.

Despite the determination everyone had that the show would go on, Billy finally had to announce to the crowd that the premiere would have to be canceled. There was some kind of retention of gas in the draperies and carpets of the theater. We went directly to the reception that had been planned.

There Billy told us that the police had found a Nazi swastika painted on the can that held the tear gas. They were picking up known members of the Nazi party. There were feelings of frustration—some of anger—some of shock in the crowd.

But then Corrie ten Boom came to the front, her trusting eyes and calm face a comfort to the hundreds of disappointed guests. Corrie is like a little child in her complete trust of her heavenly Father. She talks about the Lord as if He were her real father. What a thrill it was to see the world through her eyes. In her Dutch accent, she announced firmly, *The Hiding Place* is about God's love overcoming hate. That's why they don't want it shown. You have to overcome that kind of hate with love." And we remembered that just before the tear-gas incident, Mr. Graham had said, "This film will show us the secret of how people with Christ and with the Old and New Testaments can survive, and come out joyful and victorious in spite of suffering."

One of my greatest honors was to present to Billy Graham the

Salesman of the Decade Award from the Direct Sales Association. I think the Lord was really watching over me during that experience.

The president of the DSA had ordered a Steuben glass eagle mounted on a marble base. When he became ill, he sent the gift by courier service to me. The courier carried the box into my office on the Thursday before the Saturday I was to present the gift at the Lubbock, Texas, crusade. My secretary, Peaches, and I watched him lift the eagle out of the box. The poor man just stood there pale as a white marble tombstone. The eagle was broken!

"What are we going to do?" Peaches asked me.

I could only pray, "Lord, You know there will be thousands of Christians and seekers there. You know there will be heads of important businesses there—Rich DeVos and others. Please give us an idea for an appropriate gift."

Then Peaches went to Neiman-Marcus and found a very simple and plain Baccarat crystal cross, with the crossbeam at a bit of an angle.

"That's perfect," I said. As I hand-carried the box onto the plane, I prayed that the Lord would put words into my mouth that would be an encouragement to salespeople everywhere, that I would be able to say what the award really meant.

Then as I stood before those crowds of people, the Lord sent the perfect words.

"This was the only trophy I could think of that would be an honor to Billy Graham as the Salesman of the Master, because it so represents the Gospel he preaches—simple, unadorned, crystal clear," I said.

I really believe the Lord planned for the first gift to be broken in order that He could put those words in my mouth. I'm continually amazed at how God puts broken things together and makes them better. He even makes my blunders come out right. As Bill Bright says, "God delights in using ordinary people to accomplish extraordinary things."

Is there any wonder that I believe the Lord is interested in even the smallest details that concern us? God knows *you* by name. God never mistakes *you* in the crowd.

15
Reach Out and Grow

"Lord, You know I've got nine hundred Displayers coming to Dallas. They're going to tour my new house. If it rains and they track mud on my new carpet, I'm going to be cross. And I don't want to be."

On the way to the Sheraton Hotel in Dallas, I asked God not to let it rain. Don and I were welcoming Displayers from all over the nation who had won the right to attend the three-day Displayer Days. Not only were all nine hundred going to tour my new house the next day but seventeen busloads of them were also invited to a barbecue and tour of Don and Linda's ranch that October night.

The weather forecast gave a 50 percent chance of rain. Outside the hotel, the clouds were so heavy they seemed to press wetly against the windows.

"Reckon I should try to rent a tent and get it set up for tonight?" Don asked me when he called Thursday morning. I knew that he and Linda had already had the tables and chairs set up around a temporary stage between the barn and Don's garageful of antique cars. The ranch house is roomy, comfortable, and beautifully decorated. But there was just no way it could hold nine hundred if it rained. Yet, weren't we supposed to pray, believing?

"No, don't rent a tent," I told him. "The Lord isn't going to let it rain." Each year our prayer life is deepened as we implore the Lord to give us fair weather for our big outdoor functions!

It still looked as though it would rain that afternoon as the Displayers, wearing cowboy hats we had given them, started gathering in the hotel lobby before boarding the buses to the ranch. Then suddenly, a good, strong, Texas wind whipped through the city streets. By the time I had taken off from the Sheraton's roof in a helicopter, the sun was setting in a cloudless sky.

As I stepped out of the helicopter into Don's pasture in front of the ranch house, Displayers were snapping my picture with their cameras. There were tall ones, short ones, the slender and the plump. But these Displayers all looked beautiful to me.

Dressed in polyester denim pantsuits and the diamond rings they had won through Home Interiors sales contests, they all looked like "somebodies"—real Think Mink women. But it was not simply that their makeup was flawless and their hair done up to perfection under their cowboy hats.

No, they were beautiful because they, too, trusted the Lord. They knew that you cannot outgive God. They understood that if you do give, you receive many rewards—as well as money. Many had come to learn that the real goal was to earn in order to share. The more these beautiful Displayers shared, the more God could channel through them.

After the Displayers had photographed the wall arrangements in Don's home to their hearts' content, we all sat in the crisp, cool, *dry* October night. While we sang, we could smell the Texas barbecued beef, beans, biscuits, and corn smoking over a hickory wood fire.

"If it keeps on gettin' better and better, oh, Lord, I don't know what I'm gonna do!" was one of the favorite songs. While I autographed cowboy hats for our Displayers, I thought that there was a lot of truth in that song. If Home Interiors got any more successful, Lord, what was I going to do?

Yet I knew that the company had not prospered because Don or Andy or our area and branch managers were so smart or so good— (we could never be really good)—or because we had worked so hard. I knew that it was because of the genius of it, of God's mind working in it. Somehow God has been able to use Home Interiors to bless a lot of people.

I thought about that the next day while the Displayers toured my house. It didn't rain a single drop then, either. Now I always try to remember that "People were made to be loved and things were made to be used." I really wanted my Displayers to tour my new house, rain or shine, because these were the people who had made it possible for me to have my home.

In fact, I had moved into my new home simply because I wanted Home Interiors people to enjoy it. I had been wanting a larger home for a long time, but the attractive but small cottage Dave and I lived in was large enough for "just us." However, when Home Interiors people came visiting, or when rallies or Displayer Days rolled around, our home was inadequate for the functions. I didn't even have room for managers to stay overnight, and I really loved having them with me!

When Dave finally gave me permission to see a realtor, I soon found that builders were installing bars in almost every new house. I didn't need our money put into one of those! And then I found the perfect home—a weathered-stone, old-English-style house built back in the 1930s, nestling on three acres with a creek and trees. The rooms were much too small, and the interior needed a lot of love and care in rejuvenating it.

"I raised my family here," the elderly widow who was selling the house assured me. "And it has been a happy home." That clinched it for me.

We bought it and began a remodeling that took a year and four months. We enlarged the foyer and added an office for me and two bedrooms. We pushed out walls, added fireplaces for warmth and coziness—enlarged the family room and breakfast area to be spacious enough to hold fifty people seated. We built a redwood deck across the back where one could sit overlooking the creek and the wild tangle of native trees. We had moved into it only two months before Displayer Days 1975.

As the Displayers roamed through my home, the joy they expressed made my happiness complete. Never did I expect to live in such a home. My special "retreat" bedroom has apricot moiré upholstered walls and a blue cathedral-height ceiling, a whole wall of bookcases around a brick fireplace, and space for a cozy table and chairs overlooking the wooded area outside. It was a place where I could really be revived during early mornings—a quiet time with the Lord. My heart could only glow with gratitude for the goodness of God!

Also looking out over our private woods is the family room with its exposed beams, huge fireplace, and wall of books. Upstairs, three bedrooms invite guests with their cheerful wallpaper and warm, comfortable furnishings. Home Interiors accessories make every room homey, plus there is a view from each room! When visiting Home Interiors people use these rooms, they have their own breakfast nook upstairs for having early-morning coffee—or late-night snacks. (This arrangement also pleases our housekeeper, Maria, who has been with us for twenty years.)

One of my greatest pleasures is having room at last for all the treasures that have been given to me through the years plus the antiques I have purchased. Special gifts such as Corrie ten Boom's plate from *The Hiding Place* and Ethel Waters's gold pocket watch, engraved with "His Eye Is on the Sparrow" are in full view.

My hope is that every person who visits our home will feel love: I have learned that real wisdom is looking at people from God's point of view and sharing His love. To know Him is to love Him. And to love Him is to obey Him.

I am often asked, "How did you learn to center your life on God instead of yourself?" This question really stops me for a moment for I have not yet achieved this fully—for I still struggle with self at times —but I do know that the real *victory* only comes in self-surrender to the God who created me; to the Lord who loved me so very much that He not only saved me but has also *kept* me (He did the keeping—not I).

I have a license plate on my car which reads simply, "Mary 3." It is a reminder for me alone *(which I need)* that Jesus is *first*—others second, and Mary third.

As I wrote earlier—once a person learns how much he or she matters to God, one doesn't have to go out and try to prove to the world how much he matters.

In his book *Victory in Surrender,* E. Stanley Jones wrote:

> When you surrender to GOD—you never
> have to surrender to any one else—

I read from the great masters as well as the Bible (called by Pat
Boone the "Manufacturer's Handbook")—from the inspirational
words of Dr. W. A. Criswell, Billy Graham, Norman Vincent Peale,
Cliff Barrows, Hannah Whitall Smith (I have read her book *The God
of All Comfort* many times), Ruth Graham, Dale Evans, G. Campbell
Morgan, Dr. George Truett—I learn from everyone I can through
association, sermons, writings, cassettes—for the mind is a garden and
what we put into it will be reproduced—and I want a good crop! I
listen to gospel music by the hour—and play through the hymnbook
for my own fulfillment, as I never was fortunate enough to have
lessons.

One of the more important ways of "walking the walk—not talking
the talk" I learned from humbling experiences when Jesus Christ let
me fall on my face when I tried to do something on my own—and I
learned that I really can't do anything of lasting value without Him
—and that, as Ethel Waters once said, "God don't bless no phonies"
—My Lord knows when I'm real—and when I'm not completely
honest in motive—and He sure enough doesn't bless "fake or phony"
—at least not for me.

Once I heard Ruth Graham relate her experience when her eigh-
teen-year-old son was going to be driving a Land Rover across Europe
to deliver supplies to missionaries in Jordan and she sought an answer
to her natural anxiety from the Scriptures. Her mind turned to John
17:19: "And for their sakes I sanctify myself, that they also might be
sanctified through the truth." She could not go with her young son
—but she could sanctify herself for her son's sake.

And in the Old Testament I remembered the words:

> Sanctify yourselves; for tomorrow the Lord will do wonders
> among you.
>
> Joshua 3:5 RSV

I truly believe God is just ready and waiting to do wonders in our lives—in our homes—in our businesses—in our nation—but we limit His wonders by our own self-centeredness—concentrating on bruises instead of blessings—our own stupid lack of faith when He has such a glorious *abundance* in store for us!

One day after we had moved into our new home and we had built a charming bridge across the small stream that separated the main acreage from a little peninsula of land between that and the larger creek, the architect came in and said, "You didn't ask me to draw this, but I want to build you a little gazebo on your little island across the stream." And just like that—from no preconceived idea at all—I said, "Oh, I don't want a gazebo—I want a chapel!"

"A chapel?" said the architect. "Well, I've never seen a chapel in a backyard."

"Well, you will—for that is what I want you to design—a little brown church in the wildwood (for the trees and vines were very dense)—a chapel where it is peaceful and quiet and remote from city noises, where anyone who wishes can go and meditate, be alone, pray, and will have a stained-glass window right where the tree branches are letting the blue sky through!"

So our wonderful architect, George Sebastian, went to city hall to get a permit to build a small chapel. This caused a lot of talk at city hall. It was the first time anyone had ever asked for a permit to build a chapel in his backyard. Then officials pointed out that the city had a flood-control plan that didn't allow construction in low areas near streams.

"There probably isn't enough land that is high enough on the other side of the creek to build a chapel," George told me.

"There must be," I said. "Check the city's topography maps." The architect went back to city hall and found that, sure enough, there was exactly the right amount of land on a curved knoll where a chapel could be built.

After the last guest at Displayer Days had left, I walked across the redwood bridge through the quiet of the trees. I stood and gazed at my chapel. The little building was not quite finished, but already I could sense what it would be. Already I loved the stained-glass rose window and the high-backed antique prayer chairs which came from a French convent. Each of these wicker-seated chairs has a prayer rail on its back. Now, as I smelled the raw redwood of the interior and listened to the chattering of the sparrows outside, I just let the peace and perfection of this place seep into me.

"Thank You, God, for all of this," I prayed. "Help me to lead the women of Home Interiors in the future."

The building of a Christian business and association is always unfinished. Each new Displayer or associate must be taught the principles of Home Interiors and understand that every person is important.

Each new manager, each new supervisor, must be made to feel the philosophy that "God doesn't take time to make a nobody."

Every last associate of Home Interiors, even those who pack the orders, must catch the Think Mink spirit—to think the *best*—don't think rabbit, fox, or squirrel: Think Mink.

And our radiant beliefs must be shared. Each new day we must seek to interpret the message of Christ to the new issues and projects confronting us.

"Except the Lord build the house, they labour in vain that build it . . ." (Psalms 127:1) is one of Don's favorite verses.

No matter how much business acumen we develop, no matter how trained or professional we become, no matter how much of God's truth we may discover, there is always *so much more* that we do not know. So the challenge is always there to reach out and grow.

That year, 1975, was also the year that a new building helped me grow and gave me the opportunity to show God's love in a very "concrete" fashion.

16
Because One Woman Believed

Members of the First Baptist Church youth choir looked as if they had been whisked by a time machine straight out of 1776 as they stood in their lacy caps and tricornered hats, their calico dresses and pantaloons. The date was October 5, 1975, ground-breaking day for the Mary C Building.

Dave and I, Don, and Dr. Criswell sat on the small platform overlooking the crowds which had gathered between the two Sunday-worship services for the ceremonies.

Don's family—Linda; tall, stalwart, fifteen-year-old Joey; handsome thirteen-year-old Ronnie; and precious, auburn-haired, eleven-year-old Christi—were seated just off the small platform. Ruth, Ralph, and David could not be present but had sent a precious telegram from their home in New Jersey just hours before.

The street on which the building would be constructed had been blocked off and was filled with people—spilling out into adjacent streets. Somewhere behind the platform on which stood the TV cameraman, an ambulance wailed through the downtown city streets. The heavens sparkled like blue fireworks overhead. When the choir and the church's brass band sang a rousing praise anthem, I wanted to shout hallelujah myself!

I fought against tears as I heard my beloved pastor, Dr. W. A. Criswell, from whose sermons I have learned so much over the years, remind the crowd that the new building would be named after me.

I rejoiced to think that the Mary C Building would join the beloved old auditorium, the new Christian Education Building, and the First Baptist School. All of the other three buildings in turn would be joined in one massive spiritual plant in downtown Dallas, ministering to our twenty thousand members.

I was thrilled to think about the people who would be affected by this building in the future. The seventy-five-piece orchestra would have a rehearsal hall instead of an ear-jangling closet in which to practice. And our big choirs would have a room spacious enough for every member to have a seat even if all four hundred showed up at once—for two stories would be designated as the Lee Roy Till Music Center in honor of our former music director. The babies in the arms of the young parents standing in the crowd below would sleep in a more comfortable nursery.

All those teenagers giggling and milling around in the street were going to have a full-size gym for after-school fellowship. The gym will be named after another wonderful Christian friend, Dave Wicker. And during the day, businessmen of all faiths—or no faith at all— would be attracted to our church because we would invite them to use the gym, too.

What better gift could I ask from the Lord than that? But already this morning I had been blessed with other gifts. In the Bible class of single adults that I teach in Sunday school, the members had presented me with a scroll, promising their support in prayer and pledges for the construction of the Mary C Building.

When Jim Thomas, my associate teacher, made the presentation, I was so moved I could hardly speak. My Bible lesson that morning had dealt with Abraham and Sarah's faith in God's promises of goodness and abundance for themselves and their descendants. When I came to the verse where the elderly and childless Abraham and Sarah asked, "Is any thing too hard for the Lord?" (Genesis 18:14) I just had to answer that question with my own personal experience.

"I guess I stand here as proof that there isn't anything too hard for the Lord," I said. "I came to Dallas thirty-six years ago on one hundred dollars of borrowed money. Nobody knew me. I didn't know anybody. And today, we're having this special day."

Why did God reach down in Sherman, Texas, to an unknown girl who had so little—and bring her to this place—this day?

I had looked out on all the faces in that Sunday-school class. Most belonged to women but a few men were faithful in attendance, too. Many of these dear friends had been stung by divorce, I knew. Others had been widowed and were struggling with depression and the cares of raising a family without a husband.

How I wished that each one could really believe that God stands ready to give us an abundance of good things! The problem for most people, it seemed to me, was that the news was so good, they just couldn't accept it.

"Today my heart is full and overflowing," I had said. "God keeps His promises far beyond anything we could ever imagine.

"A long time ago I learned that I wouldn't always be good. In fact, I learned that most of the time I won't be. I won't always be sweet or smart. But I can always be *grateful.* And the Lord loves a grateful heart."

Perhaps the thing I was most grateful for that day was that so long ago I had been able to believe that God doesn't take time to make a nobody. I was thankful that the women in Home Interiors who said they "just couldn't cope" had gained confidence. I praised God that by working with a witnessing Christian company they had learned that love transforms ambition into aspiration; greed into gratitude; selfishness into service; getting into giving; demands into dedication.

Every year, because of my success in motivating Displayers, I am asked to speak before other businesswomen, church groups, and civic clubs. I frequently tell the story of Deborah from the Book of Judges: God's use of Deborah has been an inspiration to me through the years. It illustrates the truth that one person with a *belief* is equal to a force of ninety-nine who have only interest.

Deborah lived at the time that the people of the young nation of Israel were slaves of the Canaanites. The reason they were slaves was that they had disobeyed God and He had allowed them to become slaves. They didn't have kings. Instead they were ruled by judges who were wise and compassionate and learned in the ways of Almighty God.

One of the judges was Deborah. The only thing the Bible tells us of her husband is that she was the wife of a man named Lapidoth.

As the enslaved people came to Deborah with their problems, she wondered what she could do to help them. She did what every wise woman does—she took it to the Lord in prayer, and her answer came in a rather startling way.

She called Barak, the head of the Israelite army, and said, "Hath not the Lord God told you to gather ten thousand men and go up to Mount Tabor where He will deliver the Canaanite commander, Sisera, and his forces unto our hands?"

Barak answered, "I will go—if you will go with me." She said that she would go on one condition—that Barak not take credit for the victory: ". . . for God will deliver Sisera into the hand of a woman."

They assembled the forces on Mount Tabor and then Barak became discouraged. It seemed the Canaanites had nine hundred chariots of iron. In the whole Israelite army of ten thousand, there was not a single weapon!

But Deborah went to Barak and said, "Up! For this is the day that the Lord God hath given Sisera unto your hands. Hath not the Lord God Almighty gone before you?"

So Deborah and Barak led the forces. God gave the Israelites the victory. The story ends with these words: "The land had rest and peace for forty years." Think of it—the course of history changed because *one* woman believed! (*See* Judges 4,5.)

I thought about Deborah once more as I sat on the platform and listened to the ground-breaking ceremonies for the new Mary C. Building. I thought about how overwhelmed I had been when I had first heard Don announce at our Home Interiors Christmas party that the building would be named for me. And I remembered how grateful I had been to the Lord when I heard what Don told the First Baptist congregation the morning they first heard the news.

Don had taken the microphone and stood silently for a moment. Then he had said, "When I was a little boy riding the bus to church here on Sundays, I used to see my mother working two jobs just to keep food on the table." Now his voice grew husky.

"She was just so hardheaded, she said we were going to tithe. And at the time I thought, *We sure could use that money for other things.*"

Then, shaking his head as if he still could not believe it, he said, "I see now how God has taken that money and blessed us through it."

How I cherished that memory! But I could reminisce no longer. Suddenly it was time for me to turn the first shovelful of earth.

As the television cameras followed me, I walked across the narrow street through the crowds of my beloved church friends. A workman handed me a rope which would activate the starter switch when I pulled it. I pulled the rope with an enthusiastic tug! The whole machine began to chug and shake.

Twin blades grated onto the pavement. Then, with all of Deborah's determination, they bit a chunk of concrete right out of the street. The crowd cheered and clapped their hands—and as the joyful noise rose high over the downtown streets in the crisp October air, and as I smiled through my tears at the people gathered there, I hoped that they all understood for themselves that God doesn't take time to make a nobody.

I wished that Ruth and Ralph and David could have been there, too—but I was glad they had been with us in April 1975 when we had launched this building program—and I thought of my dear friend Ralph Baker. Somehow I felt he was watching, too.

As the crowd broke up, some hurrying into the large auditorium for the second worship service of the morning, the voices of the young choir members still singing floated above our heads.

And the words of that anointed music written by Bill and Gloria Gaither seemed fitting as *my* testimony:

> Something Beautiful,
> Something good—
> All my confusion
> He understood
> All I had to offer Him
> Was brokenness and strife
> But He made something
> Beautiful of my life!

And He can do the same for *you!*

17
Viva la Différence!

These were the days when every newspaper, magazine, and television show had a lot to say about Women's Lib. Everyone seemed to be telling women they needed to become hard, domineering, masculine, and cold—so that they could win more honors and compete with men in the marketplace.

This is both a tragedy and a mockery. God never intended woman to be identical to man. If she tries to be, she is actually lowering herself. The physical and emotional differences between men and women make this an impossibility. The French say, *"Viva la différence!"* Quite a few of us agree and are still praising God for those differences!

In *Women Who Win* I told of the encounter I had with an ardent feminist, while on a university panel discussing the future of women. She wanted to know why I wasn't working actively in the movement, since I was obviously convinced that women could and should be leaders. I told her then that I believed in helping women to find dignity and status through their *own* success—not through legislation.

"You are ignorant!" she shouted accusingly.

"We are all ignorant," I replied quietly, "—only about different things." My heart ached for her. Her motives were worthy, but she was going about achieving her goals the wrong way.

Just because a woman isn't aggressive doesn't mean she has to be a doormat. I want every woman to feel like somebody—because she is! Every woman needs self-confidence—to like herself—and to have poise. Women should be beautiful, feminine, charming, gracious, and wise—this is what God intended.

I am proud of being a woman and happy about the honors that were coming to me at this time. In November 1976 I was awarded the Doctor of Laws degree from Grand Canyon College in Phoenix, Arizona. I believe this honor was given to me as a result of my addressing an organization of college presidents on the subject of motivating people to support Christian education. It was a particular thrill for me because I had never had the opportunity to complete my higher academic education. And here I was marching in a procession of eminent scholars, wearing a black gown and mortar board. This honor was another reminder to me that God does give grace to the humble!

Shortly afterward I received an invitation to become the first woman to serve on the board of directors of the Dallas Chamber of Commerce. I was already the only woman on the board of the Mercantile Bank of Dallas and the Billy Graham board. And I had been the first woman on the board of the Direct Sales Association, after which other women had that opportunity.

Whenever I am the first woman member on any board, I always try to be extremely competent, always on time. I do any job I am asked to do and try to remain feminine and charming. I have found that this formula works wonders. Men still want to be treated like men, and I, for one, want to be treated like a woman. And I have had wonderful relationships with the men on all the boards on which I serve.

I have felt good about the fact that every time I have been on a board, the standard of women executives has been raised in the eyes of the men on that board. I feel that each one of us must by our actions, our demeanor, our behavior, and our dress show that we are truly liberated by God Himself. We don't have to worry about making an impression, or pushing our way through. If we honor God, He will honor us. I have been amazed at how much influence has been given me on these boards simply because I have taken this position and worked through it.

I truly believe that when a woman comes on as being aggressive and pushy, she frightens men. They feel threatened and will react most probably in an unmanly way. Fortunately I have been on boards with men who are gentlemen, who are competent, successful, and who respect me very much as a person of competence who has a commitment to excellence.

I've also learned that when God opens the doors, we are to get up and go through them—with head held high, with confidence, courage, and enthusiasm. People *like* to be around people with enthusiasm with a purpose.

So I thank the Lord for the opportunities that have been mine and the doors that He has opened for me. It has been my great joy to be one of God's truly liberated women!

18
To the Honor and Glory of God

One of the greatest thrills of my life came on January 16, 1977, when The Mary C Building was dedicated. My beloved son, Don, and our precious pastor, Dr. Criswell had put together the plans for this building two years before. The city had deeded the church a street which was no longer going to be used as a thoroughfare in return for land the church owned elsewhere. Now the beautiful red-brick contemporary building rose among the educational and parking areas and the sanctuary and Sunday-school building, much like the remaining link in a chain that makes it complete.

We had scheduled a Home Interiors Seminar to coincide with the dedication, for many of our people had contributed funds in support of the building and wanted to be in Dallas for the big event.

Over seventeen hundred Home Interiors people shared in the special, glorious, inspiring dedication service. They came from Maine to California, from Washington to Florida. Not only was a building dedicated that day, but many lives were changed and rededicated to our Lord.

At exactly 9:17 that Sunday night Don and I stood in below-freezing temperatures to cut the ribbon that officially opened The Mary C Building. The choirs sang and the chimes rang and all the people cheered. It was a momentous occasion, and my heart was filled with gratitude that God had chosen me to take part in His work.

Before the dedication, this beautiful $3 million building was short of being debt-free by $1.5 million. I had promised to match any new pledges to the building fund dollar for dollar up to $750,000, for it was my great dream that all the money would be pledged by the time we started actually using it.

How happy I was to learn that on the great high day of dedication, our Home Interiors people and members of First Baptist had responded with almost $3 million in pledges. The building would someday be debt-free and we would have an overflow to do even more for the Lord!

Included in the program for the dedication, which my competent and dear friend Ann Hood had put together, was a tribute to me that made me feel very proud. It said in part:

> Great dreams become realities only in the lives of those who dare to dream them. Mary Crowley dared, and God has accomplished great things through her. . . . She is a strong lady, full of confidence, but her strength and confidence come not from any faith in herself or her own abilities, but rather from a deep unshakeable faith in God and His ableness to uphold, sustain, and keep His promises, come what may.
>
> One of God's greatest gifts to Mary C was her generous heart, which continuously overflows in all directions, blessing everyone in its path—her family, her employees, the handicapped she hires, her friends, her pastor, her church, the beautiful people in the entertainment world, the ugly duckling who nobody else sees—her generosity seems boundless, and her joy in giving often means as much as the gift itself. . . . May all of us who have been blessed by Mary's generous heart and those who follow in years to come feel a spirit of abounding love, enthusiasm and Christian fellowship so characterized by Mary, yet so freely offered by God to all who would dare to dream great dreams and receive great blessings from Him.

Once again I thought of the Scripture from Jeremiah 9:23,24 (LB) which is in the chapel at my home:

THE LORD SAYS: LET NOT THE WISE MAN BASK IN HIS WISDOM, NOR THE MIGHTY MAN IN HIS MIGHT, NOR THE RICH MAN IN HIS RICHES. LET THEM BOAST IN THIS ALONE: THAT

THEY TRULY KNOW ME, AND UNDERSTAND THAT I AM THE
LORD OF JUSTICE AND OF RIGHTEOUSNESS WHOSE LOVE IS
STEADFAST; AND THAT I LOVE TO BE THIS WAY.

To truly know God is one of the things that I everlastingly am
working on. I want to seek to really *know* God—not just *about* Him,
but to *know* Him.

Someone had said to me the day before the dedication, "Oh, I hear
they're dedicating a building to you tomorrow."

"Oh, no," I answered, "the building is dedicated to God. They're
naming it after me."

The fact that Jesus uses even me—to me—is still a miracle!

19
Top of the Spiral

"Mrs. C, the Office of the President of the United States just called! You have been asked to go to the White House on Thursday for a conference with him and the Chiefs of Staff."

I recognized the voice. It was Peaches Mathews, calling me from my Dallas office. But I couldn't seem to grasp what she was saying. Here I was, in the bedroom of my mountain lodge on a crisp November morning, with all my thoughts and energies focused on training the twenty-five precious managers who waited for me below.

In fact, it was so early in the morning that the sun was only just now beginning to filter through the tall pine trees outside my window. I had just finished my morning prayers. I had prayed for each one of the women who were waiting to study Proverbs with me, because I wanted them to have the spiritual energy to meet the demands of home, husband, and career. I'd been asking God to help each one to learn to put Him first in their lives.

But now, here was Peaches on the phone. She seemed to be saying something about my going to the White House.

"Peaches, did you really say the President? On Thursday . . . ? Would you please run all that by again?"

"It's the Executive Office," Peaches said, her voice sounding as awed as mine. "President Carter has invited twenty-five heads of corporations from across the nation to meet with him and his Chiefs of Staff to discuss current business trends and leadership input. You are one of the leaders he has invited."

So, it *was* the President! That was wonderful, but what was I going to do? On Thursday, the day I was invited to the White House, I was already scheduled to speak to the Christian Women's Club of Buena Vista at a luncheon meeting. I had learned that over 280 women had made reservations. I realized many women in the valley needed a wonderful, exciting, positive Christian message. They needed to be made to feel like a "somebody."

Besides that, the twenty-five new managers waiting for me below were to be my guests all week, Thursday included. I couldn't just drop everything to run off to Washington!

"You'll have to tell the President I am too busy right now. See if Don or Barbara might represent us," I said hesitantly, thinking that if my son couldn't go, then Barbara Hammond, the assistant sales manager and vice-president, could take my place. I couldn't help but feel a little disappointed as I hung up.

With my mind in a whirl, I hurried downstairs to where my managers were waiting with their Bibles, tablets, and tape recorders. I looked around the room. Some of the women were still in their twenties. They had preschoolers to nurture and husbands struggling to advance in their careers. Some of the mothers had teenagers to motivate in a world that seemed to have gone topsy-turvy, yet they needed fulfillment for themselves as well. And then there were grandmothers, happily filling their empty nests with an exciting new career.

This morning we were going to talk about putting God first in their homes and business lives, but I couldn't help telling them about the phone call.

"An interesting thing just happened," I said. "The Office of the President of the United States just called Peaches in Dallas and invited me to come to Washington on Thursday. I had to tell her to say I was too busy to come," I said.

Mouths dropped open all over the room. Then all at once everyone began talking.

"You can't say no," they all seemed to be saying. "You *must* go ... we can manage ... we *want* you to go to Washington and represent us to the President."

"But how about the Proverbs study, and the speech for the Christian Women's Club?" I protested. "I can't just pick up and leave."

"Yes, you can! We'll do the program for the luncheon," they all echoed. Was it possible that their eagerness to have me attend was a sign from God that I was truly meant to go to Washington? But on the other hand, would I really do more good staying here and training them and speaking to the Women's Club? What would I do if I put God first?

"I really think we need God's guidance on this," I said. "I want to be where He wants me. Let's pray about this."

Quickly we joined hands and formed a friendship circle in front of the crackling fireplace. As I heard each of the women's voices, asking for God's guidance and blessing, I felt His wonderful peace clearing away the confusion in my mind. I didn't feel any yes or no answer, yet I felt very calm and secure that whatever the answer would be, it would be the right one.

We all sat down, opened our Living Bibles and began to discuss Proverbs and how this book of wisdom related to us as mothers, wives, and successful women. Just about the time we finished our morning session, Peaches phoned again.

"Mrs. C, the President doesn't want anyone else from Home Interiors and Gifts. He wants you," she insisted. Then Don came on the phone, speaking briefly and to the point.

"I have arranged for the company plane to pick you up tomorrow afternoon at five. You can be in Washington tomorrow night and all day Thursday, then return Thursday evening. That way you can be at the mountain for Friday."

Everything seemed to be settled, all the arrangements made. Suddenly I realized that God had answered my prayer by showing me that the decision was out of my hands.

So, on a busy Wednesday, my managers and I crammed two days' study into one. We planned the program they would lead for the Christian Women's Club. I packed my bags. By 5:00 P.M. I was on the Home Interiors jet, watching the beautiful Rockies fading into the sunset. What a day!

All of a sudden I had time to think for the first time since Peaches had called. I, Mary Crowley, was actually going to Washington, D.C., as the guest of the President of the United States! Would I ever have dreamed such a thing could happen to me back during the Depression when I first asked Mr. Jalonick for a job? Or when I was struggling to pay the children's dentist bills and learning to tithe? Or when I took the first step toward forming Home Interiors by asking a supplier to help me?

In those days, I would never have dreamed that my opinion could ever count for very much anywhere outside my own home. This trip would have been beyond my wildest imagination.

But women's lives often turn out that way, I thought sleepily, as I settled into my passenger seat. Our lives are like a spiral that starts small, but can end up big. By asking, seeking, and finding; by putting God first in our lives and working hard and believing the best, our lives spiral outward to influence more and more people, to help, to give, until finally we may even end up being asked to the White House!

How could life be any more wonderful than that?

But before I knew it, I had fallen asleep. Within a few hours I was in Washington. There was very little time, what with trying to get a good night's rest, to worry about what would happen the next day. Once again I was glad I could say to God, "You think about tomorrow. You're going to be awake all night anyway," and turn over and go to sleep.

Not until I was actually in the Oval Office myself did I really believe that I was in the White House. There I was, touching the chairs that encircled the huge, oval table, each chair bearing the name of a cabinet member on its back. How many times had I watched on television as the President signed a bill or received a prime minister in this very room?

The other twenty-four business leaders and I had met, briefly, before being ushered into the Oval Office. Now I sensed that we all felt a little nervous, even though a very dear aide to the President kept cracking jokes and putting us all at ease.

As we waited expectantly, the door suddenly opened. Instinctively we all rose to our feet as President Jimmy Carter strode into the room.

Wearing his famous smile, he shook hands with each of us and called us by name before taking his place at the large oval table.

If I had envisioned a calm, quiet chat with the President, however, I was wrong. For no sooner had he entered the room than a whole army of reporters and television cameramen marched into the room. They thrust microphones into the President's face. They shot questions at him like machine-gun fire.

How different this scene was from the orderly one that we often see on our television sets in which a public figure is shown giving a brief answer to a single question. It would be almost impossible for the President to make wise answers under such circumstances. He really had no time at all to study the questions. I felt a sense of compassion for him, and a realization that the President is human, too.

Once the press had left, we all got down to business. Each cabinet head made a short talk about his department and what was happening. Then the President spoke.

"The nation has three major problems," he told us, "unemployment, the national debt, and the energy crisis. I have called you to Washington because you are the leaders in your companies. And I would like to know how you feel your companies can help."

We recognized the problems of which he spoke, but we felt that he needed to know the problems of business, too. One after the other we corporation heads told him that there was no possible way that American businesses could save energy and at the same time expand so that more jobs could be provided.

Then we began to ask the President questions which he would refer to the proper cabinet member. But these officials did not seem to have the answers either. I was chagrined to see that none of them appeared to know what was going on outside his own department. Again I reminded myself of the many problems in our nation that stem from the bureaucracy that has grown up like some kind of monster within it. There is a tremendous lack of coordination.

"Obey the government, for God is the one who has put it there," (Romans 13:1 LB). I had to keep reminding myself that Paul said in Romans 13 that God gave us the law, and that the administration of the law is according to His plan; that all authority is from God. Yet I did not agree with everything the President had to say. He was doing his very best. But the problems were serious, and our government hopelessly complicated. Certainly our President needed wisdom far beyond his years or experience.

As the Home Interiors' plane whisked me across the breadth of our nation that evening, my mind churned. What could I do to help the President, to help the country I love? And suddenly I knew. I could always pray. I could pray that the President would surround himself with good counselors, that he would receive wisdom from above. I could pray for the President, and I could enlist others to do likewise. What wonderful changes we could see come about in America if all the millions of dedicated Christians in the United States would pray that our leaders would seek God's wisdom!

I thought again about how the course of a nation's history had once been changed when one woman, Deborah, my Old Testament model and friend, had prayed—and then acted on God's answer. I remembered how her story ended with the promise that her nation would have rest and peace for forty years.

Yes, prayers had changed the course of history. And they still could! Right away, I resolved to enlist our Home Interiors' people to pray regularly for the President and for his administration.

And I'm asking all you who read my book to do the same!

Oh, yes, I believe in prayer. But little did I realize, as I winged my way across the nation that night, that within only a couple of months, another plane would carry Don and his family to a destination in which only prayer could save their lives.

At the time I was busy thinking about helping the President, training managers to be more effective women, planning the celebration of Home Interiors' Twentieth Anniversary the next spring. It was good that I could enjoy the fullness of that day without borrowing tomorrow's troubles.

(This chapter was adapted from "A Mountaintop Experience" and "Wisdom and Common Sense" in *Women Who Win*. This totally unexpected event in my life made me realize once more that even the mighty and powerful need prayer—lots of prayer. I wanted to tell this story again as a reminder to us all that prayers *have* changed the course of history. We women of today should use Deborah of the Old Testament as our model.)

20
The Nightmare That Turned Into a Miracle

Christmas 1977, like our Lord's birthday every year, had been a very special time for me. I'd enjoyed its rush and confusion, the luscious smells of baking, the joyful sound of carolers, the eager faces of children.

I had found myself caught up in the glory of the familiar story of how God was made flesh and dwelt among us, in the lowly cradle of Bethlehem. Little did I know how soon I would have to call on this joyful knowledge to sustain me in a time of trauma for my family.

Don had flown his wife, Linda, and their sons, Joey and Ronnie, and daughter, Christi, to Montana for a wonderful family ski trip right after Christmas. My home, still filled with the beauty of holiday decorations and the echoes of our family reunion, held an unusual quiet and peace.

I was glad that Don and his family had this opportunity for a trip together. My only concern was the weather. Wednesday, December 28, the day they were to return, was rainy and dreary. The noon weather report had indicated that the poor flying conditions would clear up, but the weatherman was wrong. Fog closed in quickly in the Dallas area.

Earlier in the day Don had called to say that they were taking off in their plane from Pueblo, Colorado. They expected to reach Addison Airport in Dallas about 6:00 P.M. I knew that Don was an excellent pilot, so I didn't really worry, yet I realized that with the fog he would have to use an instrument approach. Though he had landed that way before, still there was always the chance of an accident.

When the direct line from the hanger rang about 6:30 P.M., I felt a happy sense of relief.

"Hello . . . Don, you are home!" I said.

It was not my son's voice that answered, however, but Don Breedlove's, Don's assistant.

"Well, yes, they are in, but Don landed off the runway. Joey and Christi are unhurt, but Linda is a little shook up and Don and Ronnie are scratched up some." *(What an understatement!)* "So they have been taken to Medical City Hospital. I'm on my way over there and I'll call you from there," he said.

After he hung up, I sat almost frozen for a few moments. Then I told Dave what Don Breedlove had said. I decided I would go on to the hospital rather than wait. As I drove, I was thanking the Lord for His protective shield around the family.

Only when I reached the emergency rooms did I begin to realize the seriousness of the situation. Linda was lying in one room, shaking with shock, her eyes getting blacker by the minute. Ronnie was in another room with a slash across the top of his head and a large bandage around it. Doctors were working with Don in another room behind closed doors. I knew right away that he must be seriously injured, but I was needed to comfort Christi, who was anxious and in shock—but unhurt.

Much later, while the emergency team was still working over Don in the X-ray room, and as I was standing by Linda's bed, a neurologist came in. Without a word of compassion, he started telling me that Don's condition was critical.

"There is leaking of the cranial and spinal fluid. We may have to operate on his brain immediately. If that is the case, I want you to understand that there is always the risk of infection, and that antibiotics have no effect on this type of infection."

All the strength drained out of me as the doctor spoke. A cry of protest welled up inside me, but never reached my lips. Only a few hours before, I had been talking to Don by phone. He had been fine, and my world had been safe, secure, and far beyond the pale of disaster. Now, only a few hours later, the grim reality of tragedy hovered over me like a black cloud. The lingering joy of the holiday season was erased by a wave of pain. Then a favorite Bible verse flashed mercifully into my mind: " . . . perfect love castest out fear . . ." (1 John 4:18). I could *choose* not to be afraid, for the Bible told me God's perfect love could banish fear. Prayer should be our first resource, rather than our last resort.

Summoning all my determination, I mentally cancelled out the negative words of the neurologist. I quietly placed my son in the loving hands of our Heavenly Father.

Later Don's family doctor arrived and told me that while Don's condition was critical, it was not necessarily fatal. Don was to be taken to surgery where the compound fracture of his ankle and his foot would be cleaned and set. His jaws and his teeth would be wired together temporarily, and a tracheotomy would be performed so that he would not choke on the blood from his facial injuries.

"Doctor, may I see Don before he goes to surgery?" I asked. The doctor took a quick look at me.

"Well, I don't know. He's in pretty bad shape," he said. This doctor didn't know me, and I could see he was afraid that I might break down and upset Don.

"I promise I won't cry or become emotional," I said. "I just want to pray with him."

When the doctor nodded his head, I quickly entered the room, and saw Don lying there, all broken and bloody. My heart leaped into my throat, but our dear Heavenly Father wrapped his strong arms around us both. I took Don's hand and felt his fingers clasp mine weakly. I could see him desperately hanging on to consciousness as he tried to talk to me.

Motioning him to silence, I began to pray with him. Immediately I felt the calm assurance of God's love and power strengthening and sustaining us both.

As I've mentioned many times before, what a miracle prayer is! God is so great, so mighty! Never should we be afraid to ask Him for a miracle! Again and again in His Word he tells us to call upon Him and He promises to answer. He promises never to leave us or forsake us; He promises that He is with us always; that He hears our faintest cry; that He is touched with the feelings of our infirmities; that our names are written on the palms of His hands. We are told to cast all our cares upon Him. His Word says that it is not possible for us to drift beyond His love and care. How comforting is His Word!

Later that night I was able to go home, change clothes, and freshen up a bit before going back to stay the rest of the night and day at the hospital. The doctor had told us Don would be in surgery about four hours.

About 5:00 A.M. on Thursday, Don was wheeled from recovery to the Intensive Care Unit where Linda and Ronnie were already sleeping soundly under sedation. The nurses let me stand by Don's bed.

As I listened to the sound of Don's breathing machine and the beep of his heartbeat monitor in the semidarkness of the ICU unit, I was not his "business partner." I was simply a mother standing by the bed of her son. I was praying, sometimes silently, sometimes audibly, for our Heavenly Father to save his life and mind—not just because he was so sorely needed by his family and for me and for all of us (that was my first request); but, praise the Lord, the Spirit helped me to pray for his healing that all might know that our Heavenly Father loves and cares, and that He is able—that His Name might receive honor and glory.

All through that long dawn in the ICU, I stood by Don's bed, my heart full of gratitude for his being alive. At the same time, I was wracked with pain for his hurt—seeing him lying so still, with the tracheotomy tube in his throat and other life-giving tubes attached, and with his helpless body there so broken, so painful. It was as if God spoke to my heart: "I understand, Mary, I understand—I, too, saw My Son broken and bleeding and hurt and helpless. I understand, I care, and I'm here!"

What a peace flooded my soul and what assurance flooded my spirit!

> There's not a heartache that He does not share,
> There's not a place that He is not there.

Soon messages and prayers from many friends began to arrive.

Barbara Hammond and her husband, Howard, came to Dallas that Thursday. Barbara was the one who immediately began referring to the prayers that were being said for Don as "the miracle that was heard around the world."

Billy Graham called from Johnny Cash's home in Jamaica, and I talked with both of them as they assured me of their prayers for Don and his family.

Norma Zimmer phoned: Corrie ten Boom's office called from Los Angeles: Paul Jay, a dear supplier friend, phoned from Milan, Italy; Dolph Sebell from Syracuse, New York; and Floyd and Millie Lyons by shortwave from Peru. Everyone was forming a prayer circle around the world. Truly a prayer brigade was storming the courts of heaven for help in behalf of the Carter family, and especially for Don that crucial day, Thursday, December 29. Prayer groups from the church and from Home Interiors households all over the nation held vigils for Don around the clock, as the miracle of love and prayer continued to sustain us.

My dear daughter, Ruth, came in Thursday, too. She was a tremendous source of comfort throughout that next week.

The doctors took hundreds of X rays of Don's brain, every two millimeters apart, to see if there was damage to the brain tissue. Oh, how we prayed as we watched him go from X ray to X ray. My wonderful pastor, Dr. W.A. Criswell, and Gary Moore, our minister of music, came and stayed four hours, as we waited to hear the report. As Don was wheeled by early that morning, he managed to raise one thumb up to communicate silently, "I'm gonna make it!" Praise the Lord! We are built of tough stuff!

Many hands reached out to help during those traumatic days. Don's secretary, Vickie Lay, was able to understand Don's "signing" when he couldn't speak because of the tracheotomy tube in his throat. She stayed long hours at the hospital "speaking" for him to nurses.

Don's oldest daughter, Jeanine, was able to use some of her nurse's training to stay by him, and she, too, learned some sign language.

All this time there was prayer support such as I never imagined. A dear Displayer later wrote me:

I had intended to write as soon as we heard about Don, but I knew you must be so busy and worried. Now that we know he is going to be all right, I must say that I felt all along that God was going to keep him here a while longer, for there is just too much work left to do—and too much love left to be given away. . . .

Many wonderful promises of God came to bless my heart.

"I am the Lord, the God of all mankind; is there anything too hard for me?" (Jeremiah 32:27 LB).

Many wonderful verses of promise came to comfort me.

"Call to me and I will answer you . . ." (Jeremiah 33:3 RSV). I was calling—and He *was* answering.

The miracle of prayer and love was continuing. On Saturday, the hospital changed Don's status from *critical* to *serious.* How I thanked the Lord for that milestone! Also on Saturday, Linda and Ronnie were discharged from the hospital and things began to look up all the way around. Linda's fine parents came and stayed at their home and took good care of them.

Ronnie was beginning to bounce back, too. He had had seventy-eight stitches in his scalp. Linda said she knew he was going to be all right when the first words she heard him say after coming out from under the anesthetic were "They cut my hair!" For a sixteen-year-old boy, that was traumatic!

Fortunately, the medical staff did a neat haircut. Later, at the house, a barber came in to shape his hair handsomely, and it wasn't long before he was back in school, the subject of the admiring glances of all the girls.

Christi was back to normal almost immediately, cheerleading her basketball games to victory, and playing in them, too!

Elder son Joey was the man of the house for a full two weeks. In fact, he had been the hero of that terrible night of December 28, for he had kicked out the caved-in door of the plane and gotten his mother and sister out. He had been trying to get Ronnie out when the ambulances came to help.

We were thankful that the ambulances were very close by, for Don had been pinned in the cockpit. Fuel was spewing everywhere. Another miracle: the fuel did not ignite! Praise the Lord again and again!

Isn't it wonderful that God has more resources and capabilities to draw from than we can possibly imagine? When things look bad and you're a child of God, you've always got the "checkbook." In *His* checking account are *all the treasures and resources* of heaven and earth. We need to quit thinking that God has the same limitations that we have.

Because he lives, I can face tomorrow—with hope. God is still the God of miracles, and all of us at Home Interiors shared in this one heard around the world.

I knew that when Don was whole and healthy again I was going to be grateful every day of my life. (In fact, the first thing I do every morning, even now, is to thank the Lord for the preservation of Don and his family.)

Even in the first terrible days after the accident, I began to wonder what I could do to thank the wonderful doctors and nurses for the care they were giving my loved ones. And it was remarkable how God revealed to me, in a very definite way, a tremendous need of this hospital—something that would benefit many people.

I had taken a room at the hospital while Don was in the ICU and Linda and Ronnie still hospitalized. Because it was the end of the year, I set up a little office where I could work with the CPAs when I wasn't visiting Don.

One night I had already prepared for bed. While reading Billy Graham's *Day by Day,* I realized that the devotional was talking about forgetting the past and looking forward to the future. With a shock I realized that it was New Year's Eve. And suddenly an inner voice seemed to say to me, "Go back down to the ICU waiting area and see the Coleman family."

This was the family of one of my employees, whose father was dying in the ICU unit. So I dressed and went down there. Never will I forget the pitiful scene. The family was rather large, and the balcony outside the ICU where they had to wait was tiny. Young and old, the mourners were huddled together—with no privacy, no place to be alone.

I shared some time with them, and then we prayed. But all the time I kept thinking, "Oh, there ought to be a chapel here, and chaplains, too, to bring some comfort to these people."

I talked with others in distress that night. I remember particularly one black man sitting by himself off in the corner, looking alone and anxious. I introduced myself and asked if I could be of help.

"My wife's in there," he said, pointing at the ICU. "We had a terrible accident in the car."

"Don't you have any friends or family who can come and be with you?" I asked. But he only shook his head.

"We don't live here. We were just passing through," he said. How saddened I was for that man.

This new ultramodern hospital had been developed by a group of doctors and investors. Although there was a little room on the lower floor that had sometimes been used as a chapel, it really was not conducive to prayer or providing solace for the grieving. There was no name on the door—so most people never even found it. And the hospital had no chaplains, either.

After Don was better and Ruthie had gone home, I walked into the office of Mrs. Marliese Mooney, Executive Director, one day. She was reading a letter from Ruth. Out of it fell a check for five hundred dollars. I had not known that Ruthie had written the letter or the check.

"Your daughter wants to start a chaplaincy program for the hospital," Mrs. Mooney said. "I think that's a wonderful idea." I smiled.

"That's just like my precious daughter. She and I both have wished you had a chaplaincy program here. But I think you really need a chapel, too."

Mrs. Mooney was warm to such a proposal, but she said there was no space anywhere in the hospital to put a chapel. Evidently God liked the idea, Himself, because it wasn't long before a man who leased a space right by the front door told Mrs. Mooney that she could use the space for a chapel, if she would lease him another room. And she did.

So, unknown to Don, we started making plans for a chapel. First we had to clear the project through several boards. Then we got in touch with the same architect who designed the chapel at our home, George Sebastian. We were on our way to seeing a wonderful dream come true!

Don's first time out of the house came on January 29, 1978, when he attended church at First Baptist. He still wore the cast on his leg, and because of the stitches in his face, he hadn't been able to shave. His big white beard and the scars on his face that had not yet been corrected by surgery made him look like an entirely different person. He still had his mouth wired together and couldn't talk well or eat solid foods.

Dr. Criswell's sermon that morning included the story about what Benjamin Franklin said when the U.S. Constitution was being hammered out. Franklin had noticed the chair on which George Washington sat had a sunburst on its back. When the Constitution was completed at last, Franklin stood and said, "All during this Congress I have been looking at that chair. A few times I have wondered if this is a setting or a rising sun. Now I know this will be a rising sun."

After the sermon, I was very moved to see Don wheel himself down to the front of the sanctuary to rededicate his life to the Lord. Joey went with him. It wasn't easy for Don to talk because his teeth were still wired together, but he wanted to give thanks for his life being spared.

"For me," he told Dr. Criswell, "it is a rising sun, too."

I wept tears of joy as we all prayed together. It was a very moving, precious time to me.

Later Joey became very involved in the chapel choir and last summer was elected president of it—a tremendous honor. He went with the choir tour to Russia. He played football for his school, too.

Don and his family had been members at a church in Coppell, but at this time they started attending First Baptist. What a joy to have them all become happy joyful members of our beloved church.

Yes, life went on after the accident. Christi began to excel in track. Jeanine, Don's oldest daughter, is married to David Lusk who is now one of our Home Interiors pilots. Ruthie and Ralph's son, David, went with us on an FCA trip to Hawaii. Now Ruthie is helping to start an FCA in New Jersey.

February was half over before Don was able to spend his first hour back at the office. Then it was several more weeks before the pain and weakness faded enough for him to work a full day, as he so enjoys.

The accident had happened at a bad time, because we had been looking forward to making big plans for the Home Interiors' Twentieth Anniversary celebration. We both badly needed to be in top-notch shape to make this event the spectacular success we wanted it to be.

Yet I was pleased that Don could still joke about his condition. On February 14, he wrote a message to put into the Twentieth Anniversary yearbook that said, "When they pulled the pin out of my head last week, it went from one side to the other . . . this only proves my head is hollow! I always knew there was something missing up there."

He also wrote:

> Yes, I do plan to fly again . . . I definitely believe that it is the safest way to travel, and I love it very much! We do not know yet what happened, as all the instruments were working and we were on instrument approach. The accident should not have happened, as it is the same thing that I have done many times before. I am sure of one thing . . . the Lord has shown me that if it was supposed to be fatal He would have made it that way. He saved me and my family because He knows how much I love to fly. I will fly again!

Praise the Lord! Don was going to be healed, not completely un-scarred by the accident, but healthy in body, mind, and spirit. The Twentieth Anniversary celebration would be a miracle for me not only because the Lord had caused Home Interiors to grow so large. It would also be a miracle that all of my family would be there and able to enjoy it.

21

The Twentieth Anniversary Celebration
A Tribute to the Lord

It's not often I am speechless, but on the first day of Home Interiors' Twentieth Anniversary celebration, words almost failed me. Don and I were sitting on a platform that was surrounded with sweet-smelling pink and white carnations. Dr. and Mrs. Criswell (my pastor and his wife), Billy and Ruth Graham, and Cliff and Billie Barrows were with us. From behind wafted the lovely sounds of the First Baptist choir.

Don followed me to the microphone, walking forward and standing straight, even though he used a cane. The eleven thousand Displayers, managers and their husbands who overflowed the mammoth Dallas Convention Center cheered for Don till the rafters shook. Tears of joy and gratitude were flowing down their cheeks.

Surely my cup was running over. Yes, Don was still in pain. He still had scars on his face. But he was here beside me, cracking jokes, waving to the crowd.

As the choir sang the "Battle Hymn of the Republic," I was thinking, "Yes, my eyes *have* seen the glory of the coming of the Lord."

The four months since Don's accident had been exhausting. I'd always told my Displayers, "If your purpose is worthwhile enough, and your belief in it is strong enough, the strength of the purpose will take over and keep you keeping on, even when you are physically exhausted."

To me, the purpose of the Twentieth Anniversary was not just to celebrate what we at Home Interiors had accomplished, but instead to demonstrate what God had done through the company. I was determined to give Him the glory for it all, and He gave me strength to accomplish the task.

Not only were we scheduled to have the world's greatest evangelist, Billy Graham, speaking at noon, but the next night we were to be entertained by Bob Hope, one of the most famous comedians in the world.

I knew Billy well, but I had never met Bob before, and I was determined to make his participation with us enjoyable. We sold T-shirts with Bob's picture and the words WE GOTTA HAVE HOPE! on them. Lots of our people were buying them.

While Don was in the hospital I had gotten the inspiration to give Bob something he'd always wanted—an Oscar. How many times had I heard him crack jokes about the fact that he had never received the movie industry's highest award? So I commissioned Peter Wolf to design a nine-foot Oscar which I planned to surprise him with.

After I had had the Oscar made, I was scared to death Bob would receive the real thing at the 1977 award ceremony. I sat up until 1:00 A.M. watching on TV. I had to be just a little bit glad when he didn't get one, though in my opinion he deserves one for bringing so much cheer to servicemen for so many years.

But now was no time to be thinking about Bob's Oscar. For my pastor was telling the crowd that we were probably the only convention in Dallas which began by having church services. (We had met the night before at First Baptist for worship.) "Home Interiors is that kind of company. You are that kind of people, and Mary Crowley is that kind of president," he said.

Then our lovely Queen of Displayers was at the microphone. If ever there was a successful career woman, she was it, for she had risen over thousands to reach the top in Home Interiors. Yet she was gracious and feminine enough to publicly thank a special person who had helped along the way—her husband.

How had she become Queen? It was all very simple, she said. She told how she set goals and followed the basic Home Interiors plans for success, then worked hard and tried to make all her managers, Displayers, and hostesses feel special.

"If we use the potential God gives us, we won't ever have to look back and say, 'If only I'd done this or that,' " she said. And then she went on to repeat a favorite slogan of mine.

"Through working for Home Interiors, I've learned this: 'What we are is God's gift to us; what we become is our gift to God.' "

We were further inspired when we heard Cliff and Billie Barrows tell us how we should follow the three Ps PRAISE, PRAY, AND PEG AWAY to become better wives and career women. Cliff quoted from Proverbs to say, " 'He who finds a wife finds a good thing.' I found Billie thirty-seven years ago. She halves my sorrows, doubles my joys, and triples my expenses!"

Then Kim Wickes sang a stirring witness to her faith. Blinded at the age of three by a bomb in Korea, she came to this country and received help from Cliff Barrows and Billy Graham to develop her musical talent. I could not help but marvel at the way in which God had brought victory out of tragedy for her. Her beautiful face, framed with her long black hair, was radiant with the joy of serving the Lord.

Suddenly, it was my turn at the microphone, speaking about "The Miracles of My Life." I had given a lot of thought to this speech, because I couldn't help but be grateful—and give thanks to the Lord—for all the wonderful things that had happened in my life. God didn't have to give me these gifts, but He had, freely.

First I had experienced the "Miracle of Birth"—being born in the United States to believing parents, who taught me to know God. Then I had received the "Miracle of Open Doors"—being able to come to Dallas and rear my two children with the help of the church; and being able to create a wonderful, God-serving company like Home Interiors at the very moment when I could have been crippled by the diseases of self-pity and resentment.

We had experienced the "Miracle of Sharing," made possible by God's mysterious arithmetic. We had been able to pay a bonus and a dividend during Home Interiors' very first year, even though my CPAs had said we had no reserves.

I had answered, "It all depends on what you call reserves. You call it money—we call it people."

Finally I had received the "Miracle of Prayer," when God heard the petitions from friends and loved ones all over the world and healed Don and his family.

Yes, my whole life was a miracle. As I looked at the solid sea of happy faces that filled every space in the convention hall up to the ceiling, I remembered these lines:

> If righteousness is in the heart—
>   there will be beauty in the character;
> If beauty is in the character—
>   there will be harmony in the home;
> If harmony is in the home—
>   there will be order in the nation,
> If order is in the nation—
>   there will be *peace in the world.*

Oh, how I wished that every woman there could know the righteousness, beauty, and character that comes from serving God!

Then Billy Graham was challenging us to live according to God's purposes. He pointed out our country's increasingly socialistic ideas and the self-serving attitudes of so many Americans who want to *get* more than they *give.* He described the problems that have been created by more sophisticated weapons, medical breakthroughs, and energy shortages. He criticized the breakdown of the American family.

With these problems, we are all "living on the fault line," just as Californians live on the edge of the San Andreas earthquake fault, he said.

"But we can avoid the earthquakes, we can change it all. If the United States has a spiritual awakening, we can be saved. And you in Home Interiors and Gifts can help change it all, because you go into the homes, and you can have an influence," he said.

I loved it when Billy told the audience, "Never say you're *just a housewife.* Mothers have the greatest jobs of all. They're the most fulfilling. Learn to say, 'I'm a housewife and a mother and I'm *proud* of it.' "

Then he praised his wife, Ruth, for having raised their five children virtually alone, as he had had to travel around the world so much while the children were young. "She had the Bible in one hand and a switch in the other," he said. "All five children know the Lord."

Billy had lots of tips for successful marriages: "Listen to God," he said. "Read the Bible and submit to it . . . be attractive . . . greet your husbands with a kiss . . . keep the house clean and don't gossip. Pray together with your husband. (If he won't do it, live your faith in front of him, pray for him, and one of these days he'll come around.)"

Yes, we were fed and filled that day with spiritual enthusiasm. As the crowd reluctantly left the convention hall, my heart overflowed with thankfulness. Once again I thought about Proverbs 10:22—"The Lord's blessing is our greatest wealth. All our work adds nothing to it" (LB).

Spiritual blessings we had in Home Interiors, and we also had the material ones. For the next night, when Bob Hope performed, women in fur coats and diamond rings—which they had earned for themselves—smiled out in the audience. Truly they knew the joy that comes from working hard, sharing a lot, and depending on the Lord.

When Bob marched up to the microphone, cameras flashed like fireworks. Bob, who has performed to plenty of all-male audiences, was overwhelmed when he saw the enthusiasm that can come from a mostly female one.

"I don't believe it," he kept saying, but recovered quickly to ad-lib, "I've never seen so many gorgeous gals in my life. I wish I were six months younger!"

Then he went on to say, "I realize I've made a big mistake. I should have done my TV show here."

While Bob wasn't on television, we did film the whole performance. We gave him a copy of it later on. Bob entertained the crowd royally. He even joked about not ever having received an Oscar!

Of course the high point for me was when we rolled out the nine-foot golden replica of an Oscar award, and Don Carter announced, "The winner of the Twentieth Anniversary award is *Bob Hope!*" The orchestra played "Star Wars," and Bob's face shone with amazement and joy. He appeared truly amazed. He got so excited that he actually climbed to the top of the Oscar and kissed its face.

Later he told us he was going to put it in his museum along with the pictures of our convention. No matter how big and famous people are, they still are human. They want to be treated with something special. They want to be accepted honestly and sincerely.

The crowd adored Bob. They loved the feeling of success that comes from being associated with a company that teaches self-confidence, that changes timid housewives into fulfilled women who know how to give of themselves to others, to be better wives and mothers.

> Happy is the person
> Who possesses . . .
>> *Unbounded enthusiasm for life;*
> Who practices . . .
>> *Unlimited forgiveness toward others;*
> Who expresses . . .
>> *Unending gratitude toward God;*
> Who wages . . .
>> *Uncompromising war on injustice.*

It seemed that good things would never stop happening to me during 1978. Yet, already I was making plans to receive another wonderful award.

22
Some Call It "Luck"

A letter saying that I had been selected to receive the Horatio Alger Award had arrived before the Twentieth Anniversary celebration, but I had been much too busy to think about it.

After the convention I reread Dr. Norman Vincent Peale's letter, which invited my family, friends, and most valued associates to be with me on May 15, 1978, in the Waldorf Astoria Hotel in New York, when I received the award.

Ruthie and her family were planning to attend. Don had scheduled his surgery around the date so that he could make it. Now, however, the doctor insisted he had to have a special "tunnel" operation on his foot, and that meant Don wouldn't get to see me receive the award.

So I invited my other family—my Home Interiors "sisters," and when the bronze bust of Horatio Alger was given to me, 110 of them almost filled the balcony.

The Horatio Alger Award is presented to those who have faith in the American free-enterprise system and purposeful work. They must have shared their good fortune in such a way that jobs, health, and a higher standard of living are brought to others. Their lives must be an example of how our country offers real opportunity for success.

The whole event was exciting for me. On the day I arrived in New York, I was interviewed by *Success* magazine for a future article, along with Mary Kay Ash (my old friend from Stanley, who was also to receive an award); and Wallace Rasmussen, chairman of the board of Beatrice Foods.

The next day, I was interviewed on TV along with George Shearing, the blind pianist and composer. Then, during a reception for all the new and former winners, I was thrilled to meet people like Helen Boehm of Boehm Porcelains, Lowell Thomas, and Hank Aaron.

When Dr. Peale introduced me at the banquet, he mentioned that I had not had a regular family when I was growing up. I had prepared my acceptance speech in advance. But when he said that, I felt I just had to depart from what I had written.

"Now I have a wonderful family to bring me joy—my own, plus all of Home Interiors," I said. Then I went on to accept my award by saying, "I think that one person with a belief is equal to a force of ninety-nine with only an interest. And I have a belief. I believe in the Creator who made me in His image. Because of that fact, I am 'somebody.' Consequently, I am able to look at everybody else as 'somebody,' too.

"I believe in hard work and in incentive. I think work is valuable to the person who does it, as well as to the people for whom it is done.

"I believe in women. I think women are pretty special. And I believe in America and in the free-enterprise system. I believe in the opportunities here in our country. And I know that when we dedicate ourselves to a purpose that will enrich the lives of others, and then work toward the fulfillment of that purpose, the rewards will come."

How good it was to be able to say that I was certain there would be rewards in life for those who believe that God is, and that He is a rewarder of those who believe. So many people say, "With my luck, this or that bad thing will happen. Other people get all the luck." But that's not the way luck works.

Jockey Willie Shoemaker, who also received a Horatio Alger Award, said that he had found that the more dedication with which he worked, and the harder he worked, the more "luck" he had. I'd add something else to his formula for good luck. I think you have to work *for* the good of a lot of other people, not just yourself. When you do, the rewards will surely come!

Thomas Edison said that success was 10 percent inspiration and 90 percent perspiration! Ralph Waldo Emerson said it in still another way: "If you love and serve enough, you cannot possibly escape the remuneration."

Surely my heart was overflowing. I had my Home Interiors "relatives," Ruth and her family, and even three businessmen from the Mercantile Bank with me. (Only the year before I'd been appointed to the board of this great bank, the one which gave me my first loan.)

Don sent a wonderful wire that said:

MY HEART IS WITH YOU, BUT MY BODY AIN'T. ONE FOOT
SAYS I CAN, ONE FOOT SAYS I CAIN'T. SORRY THE PEG LEG
WON.

And later on, in the company newsletter he would write, "Thanks for keeping me proud."

After all that, I might have expected to settle down to a more humdrum existence, but I didn't. In July I was invited by Fleming H. Revell Company, my publisher, to be at the Christian Booksellers Convention, where I was to present to Corrie ten Boom a portrait of herself.

I had met Corrie in Florida the year before, when I was with Billy Graham at Cliff Barrows's home. I had told them that if they were coming to Dallas, I had three extra rooms upstairs and I hoped they would stay with me. Corrie and her secretary were planning to come to Dallas to attend the prayer conference. Since they don't like hotels, they did stay with me a week. Soon afterward she was going to Florida, and then was returning for another meeting and other speaking engagements. She was booked into a motel.

"If you like, you can stay here again when you come back," I said. Corrie didn't hesitate. In her decisive tone, she said, "I accept." So, on the second visit, they stayed two weeks, until they were off to Holland.

I think Corrie enjoyed being in my home because she had plenty of room for an office. We even stored some things for her till she got back. Now I look back on those visits as God's way of giving us a method of serving and helping. What a joy it was to have her at my home! I marveled at the way she was dictating three books at once. She would sit out on the deck in the sun, her mind going like a jet airplane.

I decided right then that someone should do an oil painting of Corrie. So I secretly commissioned an artist to do one. I loved the finished portrait, and I couldn't wait to surprise her with it at the Christian Booksellers Convention.

When we unveiled the portrait, I am happy to say that Corrie liked it very much. It will be hung in the Billy Graham Center at Wheaton College in Illinois.

How saddened I was when Corrie had her strokes, and how glad I am that the idea had come to me to have her portrait done. God does often work in mysterious ways. Many times when we have a sudden urge to do something for someone, I think it is God's way of accomplishing what He wants done.

Was it also just a coincidence that *before* Don's accident he had decided that Home Interiors should construct a complete physical-fitness center in the building across the street from the executive offices? Don had thought that the center would offer employees a good way to relax and keep healthy. He had had the architects design a huge gym with two handball courts, a basketball court, tennis courts and gym-exercise equipment. The whole project had had to be shelved for lack of time while Don was recuperating. But later in the year we completed it.

Before long, Don himself was using the equipment. He made himself walk two miles a day on the track, even though he still had a lot of pain in his bad foot. He was helped greatly by being able to use the Jacuzzi on his feet.

By July 1978, he was able to make his feet work well enough to get his pilot's license renewed. Then he flew the Home Interiors' Saberliner into Big Sky, Montana, for our managers' convention. That was the same airport from which he had taken off on the day of the accident.

How grateful I was that Don continued to mend, and could be active and busy, doing the things he loved to do.

For his birthday, July 5, 1978, I gave him a surprise present. I enticed him to come to the Medical City Hospital and visit with Mrs. Mooney. When he walked in, lo and behold, George Sebastian and some of the doctors and nurses were also there. Then I gave him his present—an architect's rendering of the chapel and a little plaque telling all about it.

Don told me this was the best birthday present he could think of receiving—even if it was going to be eight more months before the chapel would be completed.

23
"Call Unto Me and I Will Answer Thee"

When the day came for the dedication of the Medical City Dallas Hospital chapel, it had already been put to use. The chapel had been finished about a month before the March 26, 1979, dedication.

A nurse came up to me before the service and squeezed my hand.

"You have no idea what this chapel means to me," she said. "After dealing all day with very ill patients, I need a place like this where I can come for a few quiet moments with God."

Those who had loved ones who were very sick had used it too, for it was the perfect place to find comfort and solace.

I love beautiful furnishings, and I had enjoyed helping George Sebastian find some gorgeous, antique stained-glass windows in amber and pale green. We covered the walls in beautiful amber and apricot silk moiré and used a soft sea-green carpet on the floor. The chairs and pews were hand-hewn, lustrous oak. From a curved, hand-carved antique, George made a lovely prayer rail for the front of the chapel.

Judy Helton, the wonderful artist who had done my portrait for First Baptist, had done a beautiful oil painting of Jesus as the Good Shepherd, seated with a lamb in His left hand and His right hand extended, saying, "Come unto Me."

On one wall of the chapel were the words of the Twenty-third Psalm. The Gideons had supplied beautiful gold Bibles. Bookmarkers with the Twenty-third Psalm were available for every person who entered. We even installed a stereo system so that those who desired might listen to hymns.

The chapel was located right at the front door of the hospital, in the main lobby, on the way to the cafeteria, so that it was easy to find.

The hospital's own chaplaincy program which we had established was already operating too. Young men from the Criswell Center for Biblical Studies who were trained in how to minister to people who were ill, who were hurt, who were in grief over the loss of a loved one, were on duty from 9:00 AM to 9:00 PM, and on call during the night.

Before the dedication I sat quietly alone for a moment in the chapel. How grateful I was to all those who had helped make it possible. Many Home Interiors people had contributed. And how wonderful it was that through Don's accident, God had revealed to us the need to build a chapel that might minister to thousands over the years.

So many people in this world are hurting! Some are the walking wounded. Some are distressed. It seems sometimes to me that there is a cry coming from every person. "Is there a word from God? Is there a word of comfort? Is there a word from Calvary?" they ask. And then I see Christ on Calvary and the love that was poured out there and all humanity takes on a new color. Every person can become somebody, every hurt can be healed, every burden can be lifted, every wanderer can come home. How beautifully this chapel expressed this feeling!

Then suddenly everyone who was to take part in the dedication was here—Don and his family; Dr. Criswell; Dr. Paige Patterson, president of the Criswell Center for Biblical Studies, Dr. Leon Simpson, the chaplain supervisor; and Mrs. Mooney.

The program read:

IN GRATITUDE TO GOD FOR PRESERVING THE DON CARTER
FAMILY AND IN APPRECIATION TO THE DOCTORS AND STAFF OF
MEDICAL CITY DALLAS HOSPITAL, THIS CHAPEL IS DEDICATED.

The ceremony was simple, quiet, and reverent. Each of us said a few words. I told the story of the beginning and the completion of the chapel. And then Don had a response to all the people. He spoke from his heart about God's loving care for him, expressed through the doctors and nurses.

Then Joey, representing the family, heartwarmingly thanked the nurses and doctors for their loving, tender care and gave gratitude to God for His blessings on us and His preservation of the family. How proud I was to hear my oldest grandson dedicate himself to the work that God had yet for us to do.

As Joey spoke, I was reminded again that out of every disappointment, every heartache, God can make something that brings honor to Him and blessing to others.

But it was Mrs. Mooney who expressed what the chapel really means better than anyone else. I received a letter from her that said:

Those worried about loved ones . . .

Those torn by conflicts . . .

Those needing strength to face the unknown . . .

Those wanting solace and inspiration . . .

Those overflowing with relief and joy . . .

Those thankful for miracles . . .

Those now content to know Medical City has a chapel for employees, patients and families . . .

Those—we among them—will use the chapel; each time it is visited by mankind, now and in the years to come, there will always be the thankfulness such a special place is here.

How very Christian you are to give strangers a place to pause before God . . . "I was a stranger, and you took me in. . . ."

How very generous you are to provide a fitting and inspirational dedication of the hospital chapel.

How very blessed are all of us who know you.

Thank you, Mary Crowley.

God bless you,
MARLIESE E. MOONEY
Executive Director

Once again I thought of the Scripture that had meant so much to me at the time of Don's accident. "Call unto me, and I will answer thee, and shew thee great and mighty things, which thou knowest not" (Jeremiah 33:3); and also "I know the plans that I have for you . . . plans for welfare and not for calamity to give you a future and a hope" (Jeremiah 29:11 NEW AMERICAN STANDARD).

Surely the best way to find yourself is to lose yourself in something bigger than yourself!

24
"You Can Too"

Mary C. Crowley, because of the superlative personal development influence you have wielded in the lives of thousands of your fellow women, because of your most stimulating influence on religious institutions and especially because of your magnificent generosity to Dallas Baptist College, this institution honors itself by conferring upon you the degree of Doctor of Humanities [D.H.].

The words were those of William E. Thorn, president of Dallas Baptist College, on whose board of trustees I had served for nine years. As this new college struggled to grow, it had been our joy to give it three-quarters of a million dollars, plus $100,000 in scholarship funds used by the sons and daughters of Home Interiors employees and others.

As the brightly colored hood was draped over my shoulders, I was feeling proud, yet humble and somewhat awed, for I was scheduled to give the commencement address as well.

As I wrote the speech, I had wondered what I should say to inspire young people entering a world where faith is tested by dishonesty on the job and deteriorating standards of conduct. I had thought of nothing better than the words of Scripture which have been the testimony for my own life:

O Lord, you alone are my hope; I've trusted you from childhood. Yes, you have been with me from birth and have helped me constantly—no wonder I am always praising you! My success—at which so many stand amazed—is because you

are my mighty protector. All day long I'll praise and honor
you, O God, for all that you have done for me."

Psalms 71:5–8 LB

And so, as I stepped up to the microphone, I told them how I had
been raised to know that Jesus loved me whether I was bad or good;
how I had made a commitment to the Lord at thirteen and used the
Bible as my textbook; how I had selected Deborah as my Old Testament model and Lydia in the New Testament.

And I told about establishing Home Interiors with the belief that
women are special and with the goal of building a business where
women could become professionals and still have a home, a husband,
a family, and their priorities in order.

Then I told about how one of Home Interiors' basic goals was to
give honest and sincere service.

"You see, Jesus said the only way to greatness was *to serve*. I am
speaking here now of serving through our business—I'm talking about
serving throughout life. And so, to all of you, I would say, 'Do you
want to be great?' Well, the only way to greatness is *to serve.*"

It is not just graduating seniors who must make the choice either
to strive for status or seek to serve. We must all make choices. We
do this every day—sometimes every moment. Who will be our Master? Jesus—or self? Jesus provided an example when He washed the
feet of the disciples. He did something they were not willing to do for
each other. We must choose to serve Christ so that we understand
serving each other.

Then, I shared with the seniors thoughts from Dr. Leighton Farrell
about the cost of service. If they did want to serve, they should
remember that there are four ways it will cost them.

First, *it costs time.* I do not believe that you can go to the lake on
Sunday morning and teach a Sunday-school class, or sing in the choir,
or be in your place of duty. All of us are very busy people. We have
to ruthlessly cut out the secondary things that would obstruct the
primary things. When you say *yes* to God, you automatically say *no*
to some other things. We must set priorities.

The second thing service will cost is *peace of mind,* or, as Dr. Francis Schaeffer calls it, "personal peace." I know of no painless way of serving your church or community. Sometimes we find joy and the satisfaction of success. But on the other hand we also face criticism, misunderstanding, disappointments, disillusions, even spiritual anguish. Many times we don't receive any gratitude. Often we appear to have failed bitterly in the eyes of others.

The story is told that there was a man who had given his life to the ministry of the suffering people of the inner city of London. "Why don't you run away from it all before you are broken by this inhuman burden?" a friend asked.

"I would like to run away—but a strange loving Man on the cross won't let me," he replied.

That same strange, loving Man on the cross won't let us escape the responsibilities of the Christian faith laid on us either. Somehow when we catch a vision of the cross, all humanity takes on new color. We see the possibilities of redemption everywhere. Everybody is somebody, God doesn't take time to make a nobody! And we become excited, renewed, inspired, ready to serve again.

The third thing that service costs us is *part of our selves.* It costs a part of who I am, my very life itself.

I tell our Home Interiors managers that we have time, energy, attention, and money to share. How we set our priorities in these areas will determine our success. And so we set our goals. We schedule time for family devotions, prayer life, and caring for others.

And fourth, service will cost you *a great deal of inconvenience.* If one expects that being a Christian means that life can be molded around our own convenience, schedules, and desires, I think that one has misunderstood the Christian faith. We probably will never understand the true nature of service in God's kingdom until we have learned to give up something to be a part of it. The fellowship of God's people is a privilege that excites us, a purpose that unites us, a principle that guides us, and a power that enables us. Oh, how exciting to be part of it!

Then I looked out into the faces of the graduates who were entering an exciting new part of their lives and I told about the two little silver shovels I wore around my neck. One was a little bitty one and the other was bigger. A graduate of Dallas Baptist who later entered the seminary, gave me the shovels. He had them made by his brother-in-law, who is a silversmith, when he went home to South Africa.

He told me he had heard someone ask a great philanthropist how he could give away so much and still have so much left. The man answered, "It's like this. I shovel it out and God shovels it in. He has a bigger shovel than I have."

How I hoped that all the graduates—and all of us—would learn to better share and to better serve! How I desired that we would all learn to lean on God, so that every person could go out into the world, confident, unafraid, filled with a "You can too" attitude.

This *is* possible. God does do major things that are considered impossible.

I can do all things through Christ. . . .

You can too.